# Rental Houses

## for the

# Successful
# Small Investor

Suzanne P. Thomas

Gemstone House Publishing
PO Box 19948
Boulder, CO 80308

The following trademark appears in this book: Monopoly

*Rental Houses for the Successful Small Investor*
Copyright © 1999
First Printing 1999

### Publisher's Cataloging-in-Publication
### *(Provided by Quality Books, Inc.)*

Thomas, Suzanne Patricia, 1965-
    Rental houses for the successful small investor /
Suzanne P. Thomas. -- 1 st ed.
    p. cm.
    Includes index.
    Preassigned LCCN:98-93388
    ISBN: 0-9664691-0-0 (case bound)
    ISBN: 0-9664691-1-9 (soft bound)

    1. Real estate investment. 2. Real estate invest
    ment--Finance. 3. Real estate management.
    4. Rental housing--United States. I. Title.

HD1382.5.T46 1999                     332.63'24
                                      QBI98-1264

Readers are encouraged to contact the publisher with comments and suggestions for future editions of this book.

The author is available for speeches and mini-seminars on real estate investing. Requests may be sent through Gemstone House Publishing.

# Acknowledgements:

Many professionals shared their expertise to help make the material contained in this book as accurate as possible.

Rich Levy and Andrew Ogden, 1031 tax deferred exchange specialists, read the chapter on exchanges after each revision and made many suggestions and corrections. They can be contacted by calling (800) 850-1031 or by visiting their web site at www.exchangeservice.com.

Staff at World Savings and Washington Mutual reviewed the material relating to adjustable mortgages and portfolio lenders. They went far beyond the usual definition of customer service for this appreciative customer.

Rich Schad of Farmers Insurance in Louisville, CO, checked the information regarding insurance. He has also provided me personally with excellent service over the years as my insurance agent.

Family is reputed to be ill equipped to act as editors because they will love unconditionally anything written by a member of their clan. The sources of these rumors have never met my family. Thanks for the many hours of critiquing and copy editing. It was easier to face all the red ink when I knew the wielder of the pen did so with the best of loving intentions (and amazing accuracy).

Finally, thanks to my many students. You taught me what you wanted to learn, and your feedback has made this book much more effective.

# Warning/Disclaimer

This book is provided as a helpful tool for the small real estate investor. The reader acknowledges that the publisher and author are not providing legal or accounting services, nor any other professional services.

Real estate investing is a wonderful opportunity for the small investor, but it is also possible for the investor to lose money. Events beyond the publisher's or author's control such as economic changes and local market conditions can cause financial losses.

The reader assumes the responsibility for both success and failure in his or her investing decisions. The reader should consult experts such as real estate agents, attorneys and accountants. Other books are also available on the topic of real estate investing.

Every effort has been made to verify the information given in this book. However, there may be inaccuracies. Therefore this book should be used only as a guide. All information should be double-checked by investor.

Neither the author nor the publisher shall have liability nor responsibility to any person or entity for any loss or damage stemming from reliance on the information provided in this book.

# Table of Contents

Return Example <> A 30% Rate of Return Compounded <> Where to Save Your Money <> Decreasing Rate of Return <> Increasing Your Rate of Return <> When to Restructure Your Investments <> Ignoring Rates of Return

Building Up Equity <> Saving Money <> It's Impossible to Save <> Unexpected Money <> Get a Partner <> Borrowing Money <> Taking a Breather <> Moving <> Potential for Appreciation <> Local Regulations <> Taxes and Insurance <> Inheriting Money <> Life Insurance <> Settlements <> Lease Options

Single Family Homes <> Different Types of Single Family Homes <> Brand New Houses <> Overly Expensive Houses <> Functional Obsolescence <> Getting a Discount <> Condominiums and Townhouses <> Duplexes, Triplexes and Four-plexes <> Apartment House <> Falling in Love <> Fixer Uppers <> The One Percent Rule <> Rates of Return <> Rent-to-Property Value Ratios <> Deciding Between Two Available Properties - The Shortcut Method <> Magic Price Point <> Properties with Two Bathrooms <> Moving to a Different City or State <> Buying in a Different State <> Looking with an Agent <> Helping Your Agent <> Buyer's Agent <> What If Your Agent Doesn't Do a Good Job?

**Chapter Eleven**

# 1031 Tax Deferred Exchanges

Personal Residence Versus Investment Property <> To Exchange or Not <> Why You May Want to Sell Your Property <> Taxable Gain Adjusted Basis <> Loan Amounts and Taxable Gain <> To Exchange or Not to Exchange <> The Rules for 1031 Tax Deferred Exchanges <> Selecting a Qualified Intermediary <> Identifying Your Replacement Properties <> Identifying Replacement Properties <> 180 Days to Close <> Reinvesting All of Your Proceeds <> Carrying Over Your Basis <> The Reverse Exchange <> The Improvement Exchange <> Contract Provisions <> Summary

# Introduction

This book is designed to help beginning and small investors achieve financial independence through owning a handful of rental houses. Perhaps you are just beginning to explore the idea of investing in real estate or maybe you already own a couple of rental houses. In either case, this book will help you to succeed. Small fortunes and big fortunes are made in real estate by thousands of people every year in America. You can be one of these people.

Yes, you'll have to learn a lot. You will need to know how to manage tenants, how to choose the best loans, and how to decide if a property is a good one to buy. But you can learn as you go with this book to help you along the way.

Buying and owning real estate can be fun and profitable. I'll share my guidelines for minimizing the headaches so you can relax and enjoy the financial rewards. For example, you don't have to spend weeks searching for distressed sellers or investigating foreclosures in order to do well in real estate. It's possible to pay market prices for single family homes in great condition yet still be able to rent them for a positive cash flow.

Investing in real estate is one of the best second jobs you can create for yourself. Eventually, when you've acquired enough houses, it can become your main job. Say good-bye to working nine to five!

Owning and managing a few rental houses is also a great career for the stay-at-home parent who wants to contribute substantially to the family's financial future. Compared to starting most small businesses, buying and renting single family homes involves a low degree of risk. Financing is readily available, rents can be accurately projected before you invest, and houses can be sold relatively quickly if you change your mind or move. Compared to other small businesses, it's easier to start off on a small scale by buying just one or two houses.

Investing in single family homes requires only a modest investment of your time. Each property, if bought according to the suggestions in this book, will require an average of two to three hours per month including time spent driving and doing paperwork. Though you may spend eight or ten hours in a month when you are showing a property to prospective tenants or staining a deck, other months you'll do nothing except collect the rent and pay the mortgage. Shopping for properties to buy is actually the most time-consuming activity, and you can opt to do that only when you have extra time in your schedule.

Owning real estate involves more than investing your time. You also need to know how to handle tenants, evaluate properties, stay on the correct side of the law, and more. Besides covering all these basics, this book also contains valuable tips.

For example, did you know that you can insure yourself against the possibility of a tenant trashing one of your properties? Some insurance policies will consider damage beyond normal wear and tear to be vandalism. The insurance company will reimburse you for your costs, including any lost rent during the time it takes to have your property repaired. I'll tell you what type of policy provides this coverage.

Perhaps you would like to make some money when you buy by getting a house at a small discount. I'll tell you about the type of sellers who will almost always give you a break in the price if you'll do one small favor for them. In addition, I'll tell you how to get a builder to give you a five to seven percent discount off the price of a brand new house, even if your local market is hot.

Since we all know the real estate market can go down as well as up, I'll tell you what you can do to protect yourself against the downturns. You'll find out how much equity you need as a cushion, what happens when you prepay an adjustable rate mortgage versus a fixed mortgage, and how to decide if the rent-to-property value ratios in your area are attractive.

Real estate investing can be your ticket to early retirement. Only five properties may be enough to provide you with a core income within five to ten years. You'll then be able to devote the majority of your energy to other interests besides a regular job.

Perhaps owning rental real estate will allow you to become a full-time volunteer who makes a difference in your community. Maybe you want the chance to write or paint without worrying about whether or not you'll earn enough to support yourself. Or you may want to turn your rentals over to a management company and take off to travel the world.

This book can help you realize your dreams by showing you how to use rental real estate to achieve financial independence. Every major aspect of being a property owner is covered in detail. Each chapter stands alone so you can flip immediately to the topic that interests you the most. Or you can start at page one and read straight through. Owning a handful of rental houses has given me the freedom to do what I want to do in my thirties, and I'm eager to share how I did it so you can become as successful as you want to be, too.

# Chapter One

# As Rich as You Want to Be

When I ask people why they want to invest in real estate, they usually tell me they want to make money. They dream about retiring early. They want to save for their children's college educations. Or perhaps they hope to increase their feelings of security by increasing their net worth.

When I ask how much money it will take for them to achieve their goals, they frequently say a million dollars. After all, who wouldn't want to be a millionaire? But they don't really know if a million is too much or not enough.

Before you can set your financial goals, you need to know what your dreams are. Just having money by itself won't make you happy. If you can identify what would bring you the most pleasure, then you can learn how to calculate the minimum amount of income you will need to live the way you want. You will be able to set a financial goal which has genuine meaning for you and use real estate investing to help you achieve it.

## Identifying Your Dream Life

To help you identify the life that would be ideal for you, I'm going to share with you the dream lives of two other small real estate investors as well as my own personal dream life. As you read the details of what each person would consider a perfect life you will find yourself agreeing or disagreeing. Both reactions are beneficial because they will help you to clarify the sort of life you wish to create for yourself.

**Shelley**

Shelley has two daughters under the age of ten. It is extremely important to her to be able to stay at home to raise her children. Managing her family's rental properties has proven to be a good home-based business for her, but she dreams of the day when her husband can afford to quit his job as a computer programmer. She thinks he would be happier making a living in a different way because Brandon is a man who takes satisfaction in working with his hands. He enjoys the physical effort involved in maintaining houses and would like to become an inventor.

Brandon's job is in Texas so that's where the family lives, but Shelley would prefer to live in her home state of Colorado. She is close to her side of the family and wants her children to know their cousins and aunts and uncles as more than friendly strangers. Shelley's ideal life would include moving back to Colorado before her children become teenagers.

Shelley dislikes how the family vacations currently must be scheduled months in advance. It is impossible for her and her husband to make vacation plans without receiving prior approval from his manager for time off. She wants to be able to travel on the spur of the moment, taking advantage of short notice travel bargains and going away for as long as it suits her.

Shelley doesn't mind the idea of working at a part-time job to help make ends meet after Brandon leaves his computer programming job, but she does want the financial freedom to quit any job she takes if she becomes dissatisfied with the way her employer is conducting business.

## Milt

Milt lived an unconventional life during his twenties and thirties. He did volunteer work for hospice programs and environmental groups, and spent time in monasteries. He was never a company man. He didn't like regimentation and couldn't see himself retiring after forty years with a gold watch. Since he lived a simple life a series of short-term jobs satisfied his limited income requirements.

Then in his forties he became a father. Before this happened he had been able to quit a job and travel whenever the urge struck him, but suddenly he had an obligation to support and nurture a little girl. Because he had never cultivated a conventional career he found himself with a relatively low paying job in the social services field.

Milt dislikes the pressure of having to work. He wants to regain the freedom he used to enjoy as a young man. He values having time to study and take classes. He would like to go on meditation retreats, and he wants the opportunity to do volunteer work again.

Milt sees real estate investing as his best chance to get his financial act together. He compares owning rental real estate to playing Monopoly® in the real world. He enjoys the challenge of finding loans available to a person with a low income. Barely seven years after buying his first house, Milt has turned his initial down payment of $40,000, obtained primarily as a small inheritance from his parents, into $260,000 worth of equity in four properties.

Milt doesn't have a set income goal or a target number of properties he hopes to buy, preferring instead to evaluate his situation as it evolves. He has reduced his work hours down to thirty per week and looks forward to eventually forming a community where he can live with friends who share his interest in developing their spirituality.

### Suzanne

My first job after college was okay as jobs go, but sometimes I felt like I was going to the dentist when I turned my car into the parking lot. I hated having to be somewhere at the same time every morning. An hour for lunch was too short and five o'clock came way too late every afternoon. Forcing myself to fit into the forty hour work week seemed to cause actual physical pain.

When I became a real estate agent my work schedule became deceptively more flexible. True, I could choose when to work, but if I wanted to earn a living I had to be responsive to my clients' desires. If an offer came in on one of my listings, I needed to present it as soon as possible and at my clients' convenience. If a house came onto the market that sounded ideal for one of my buyers, off we went to see it based again on my clients' availability. If relocation clients came to town for a three day house hunting trip, I had to devote myself to staying by their sides for fear that they would wander off and buy a house through another agent.

Taking a vacation was like making a deal with the devil. If an agent watched my business while I was gone, then I had to return the favor. If having one unpredictable schedule was bad, juggling a double load of clients was even worse, especially when I didn't know these new buyers and sellers. The price for going on vacation seemed terribly high.

I dreamed of a quiet, reflective life with plenty of time to read books, visit with friends and relatives, plus the leisure to write romance novels without worrying about whether they would ever sell. I wanted to garden and to learn to paint watercolor pictures of cats and flowers. I longed to be able to sleep late in the mornings, to take naps in the sunshine in the afternoon, and to stay up past midnight without having to suffer the next morning when the alarm clock went off. As a matter of fact, I wanted never again to be woken by the nasty buzzing of an alarm. If I didn't see the sun rise for the rest of my life, that would be fine with me. Sunsets and moonrises would suffice, thank you.

## A Dream Income

In the early nineties my dream income was $40,000 per year. With that type of money I could pay for all the necessities as well as a few nice luxuries such as fresh flowers and monthly massages. I wouldn't have to work at a job unless I wanted extra money to pay for something special.

One afternoon I thought about how much income my personal residence would produce if the mortgage were paid off and the house rented out for a fair market rent. I multiplied this rent amount by twelve months, subtracted expenses such as taxes, vacancy, insurance and maintenance costs, and came up with $8,000. If I owned five rental houses, each producing an $8,000 yearly income, then I would receive my $40,000 dream income.

It seemed remarkably simple. All I had to do was buy five more houses like the modest 1,300 square foot house I already owned, concentrate on paying off the mortgages, and I could retire. I thought it would take me quite a while to pay off my loans, maybe twenty years, but even so I would be retiring in my forties. That sounded more appealing than waiting until I was sixty-five or seventy.

## What Is Your Goal?

Your financial goal is inextricably tied up with your dream life. Hopefully you were inspired by the sample dream lives mentioned earlier in this chapter. Do you want to live near the beach? In the mountains? Do you want to devote yourself to volunteer activities? Run for political office? Become an artist? Learn to play a musical instrument?

Draw up a budget that matches your dream life. What is the minimal amount of income you would need to live the way you want to live? Maybe you would like to continue working on a part-time basis. How much would that contribute to your bottom line? How much income will you need to earn from your investments?

Let's say that you and your spouse determine a $65,000 income would allow you to live a dream life. You are both willing to work part-time as part of your dream life and calculate that together you would bring in $15,000 per year. You also own some stocks which would produce $5,000 in dividends per year. Subtracting your part-time work income and stock dividends from your target income of $65,000 leaves $45,000 in income that must come from new investments.

## You Say You Really Do Want to Be a Millionaire

For some people their dream lives involve fantasies of being incredibly rich. They have gone on tours through expensive homes. They imagine themselves living in one of these houses and needing a four car garage for their Mercedes, BMW, Corvette and motor home. Their clothes will fill a closet the size of their current master bedroom. A maid service will clean the mansion weekly and a gardener will keep the yard in tip-top condition.

This is a lovely fantasy, but I bet you would enjoy a different life which is tied to your true values much more. I don't think it would be worth selling your entire life away to earn these types of luxuries. Who cares about impressing friends and family plus an enemy or two with your wealth if you had to sacrifice your life to earn it?

Instead of retiring in ten years, you might have to wait thirty years. Will the extra income be worth selling away an additional twenty years of your life? Or would you prefer to live on less and do what you want with your time much sooner? Nothing is more valuable than the limited minutes, hours, days and weeks of your life. Your investments should empower you to live a life full of personal meaning, not enslave you in pursuit of the "American dream".

# How Much Is Enough?

The question you need to answer is how much money is enough to fulfill your needs and allow for the extras that make life fun. Where do you get the most happiness for each dollar earned and spent? This idea is explored in detail in the book *Your Money or Your Life* by Joe Dominguez and Vicki Robin. If you need help determining what would truly be enough for you and your family, you should read this book.

Another book you might want to read was written by two of Joe and Vicki's students, *Getting a Life* by Jacque Blix and David Heitmiller. Unlike Joe and Vicki who enjoyed a life so frugal that many Americans may have difficulty imagining it for themselves, Jacque and David take a more middle-of-the-road path. In this book they share their multi-year process of deciding what they most valued and how much income they needed to live personally fulfilling lives.

# Becoming Self-Employed

Many people dream of self-employment, either because they are the independent type or they are tired of being transferred by a big corporation. They decide to either start a business from scratch or to buy a franchise. Either choice involves a degree of risk and a certain amount of capital. The investment of time can be all consuming. New business owners tend to work many more hours for themselves than they ever did for a past employer.

Becoming a business owner poses problems daunting enough to cause any sensible person to reconsider the idea. Investing in a business is tantamount to buying a job, but unlike a normal job, it's not possible to easily quit. Someone must be located who is willing to buy the business. Otherwise the invested capital is at risk of being lost.

Self-employment can turn out to be less flexible than regular employment. There is the issue of employees. In the current tight job market it can be a struggle to find employees, and once found and hired they must be trained, managed and retained. If someone quits or doesn't show up for work, the owner is the back-up staff.

Buying a franchise is supposed to protect the new business owner from many of the risks of owning a business, but franchise opportunities can be part of fads which sweep the country. Remember when yogurt shops were all the rage? Then came bagel stores and coffee shops. Some other businesses will be hot in the future. Meanwhile a number of the old businesses will have closed their doors without ever becoming financially successful.

The problems of the small business owner put the problems of a property owner into pleasant perspective. Instead of employees who must be dealt with every day, the property owner has a limited number of tenants. Besides doing occasional maintenance, screening new tenants, showing properties, and reminding tenants to pay the rent on time and water the lawns, the property owner has little contact with the people who are paying money to him or her every month. The average single family rental property requires an average of only two to three hours of time per month to manage based on my personal experience.

Investing in real estate can be done one small step at a time. Instead of quitting a steady job to open a business, you can keep your regular job and buy your first rental house. If that goes well, a second house can be purchased and so on. If at any time you decide real estate is not for you, it is relatively easy to sell your investments. It is much easier to dispose of unwanted real estate than it is to sell a small business. Single family rental properties can be sold to homeowners as well as to investors.

## A Great Home Business

You may want to work out of your home. Books exist which describe the various types of services and products that are suitable to sell from the home, but owning rental properties is usually overlooked. This is a mistake.

Managing a rental property requires very little in terms of space. Mortgages can be paid each month when you pay your other bills. A notebook can hold your receipts and records. An extra can or two of matching paint for the rental properties can be stashed in the garage. Your personal telephone will be adequate for the limited number of calls you will receive on "For Rent" ads. Even if you include a computer for record keeping, your total space requirements will be less than two cubic yards.

Despite requiring so little room in your house, your rental property business can be worth a lot of money. Five houses worth $150,000 apiece add up to three quarters of a million dollars. This fact is especially important to the parent who chooses to stay at home with children. While the other spouse is out in the work force gaining new skills and earning promotions, the at home spouse is also developing new skills and making a significant contribution to the family's financial picture.

## Figuring Out How to Succeed in Real Estate

Until the key moment when I set my goal of acquiring five houses (a goal I eventually surpassed far sooner than I would have imagined possible), I wasn't entirely convinced I wanted to invest in real estate. Sure, I had been reading books on how to do it for years, but finding great deals and desperate sellers was considerably more difficult than the authors of these books made it sound. I did buy a couple of HUD and VA foreclosures, fixed them up and resold them, but the profits were soon spent on my living expenses.

Then I purchased a foreclosure house for a great price, at least 30% below market, and I used no money of my own to buy the house. It was a no money down deal with a catch. My partners with the cash received part of the profits. So did the previous owner of the house since I felt she deserved some of the equity. My final share of the proceeds when the house sold was less than $15,000. That money, too, soon disappeared as I spent it toward living expenses. Not to mention that it required over a year and a half to find this one foreclosure deal.

During this time period I became a licensed real estate agent, thinking that maybe all the good deals were being snapped up by the people in the business. As an agent I did learn about marketing houses, negotiating contracts, and prospecting for clients, but I did not find any great deals.

## The Power of a Goal

Once I set my goal to own five houses, I realized I had to stop buying and selling properties for a short-term profit. Holding them for the long term was what would gain me my financial freedom. During the next seven years I managed to buy an average of one house per year. Once I learned what to do, it was easy to surpass my goal of five houses.

I also changed my target retirement age. In order to buy my first five investment houses, I had been forced to get investor loans with adjustable interest rates because fixed interest rate loans for investors weren't available in the early nineties. I was concerned about interest rates going up so I protected myself against this possibility by prepaying a bit extra each month on each of my mortgages.

# Prepaying an Adjustable Rate Mortgage Versus a Fixed Rate Mortgage

That's when I learned something marvelous about adjustable rate mortgages. The payments for adjustable rate mortgages are usually adjusted once per year. When the lenders do the adjustments, they change more than the interest rates. They also check that the monthly payments will pay off the loans at the end of the original thirty year loan period, neither sooner nor later.

If you have an adjustable rate mortgage and the interest rates haven't changed over the past twelve months, then the required principal and interest payment will stay the same for the next year. But if you have been prepaying extra principal, then the lender must reduce the required mortgage payments in order to make the loan last the full thirty years of its original term.

This is different than the way it works with fixed rate mortgages. If you prepay on a fixed rate mortgage, the principal and interest payment stays the same (though the portion for taxes and insurance may change as the years go by), while the time period for the loan is shortened. If you make one extra principal and interest payment every year, your loan becomes a twenty-three year mortgage instead of a thirty year mortgage, but your loan payment never becomes smaller.

Because I was prepaying on my adjustable rate mortgages during the nineties, a time of stable or dropping interest rates, the lenders reduced my mortgage payments for my adjustable loans each year to keep me on the full thirty year loan schedule. In the meantime my rents were slowly going up. Higher rents and smaller mortgage payments resulted in an increasing monthly cash flow. I used that additional cash flow to pay down my loans even faster.

It didn't take very big prepayments to set this wonderful cycle of decreasing mortgage payments into motion. For example, if my rent was $1,000 and my required minimum mortgage payment was $660, I would pay $750, or only $90 extra each month.

Yet over five years prepaying a little every month added up to a big increase in my monthly cash flow.

For example, if interest rates on all my adjustable loans stay constant for one year and my prepayments on the loans cause each payment to drop by only $20, the total cash flow increase is substantial. Twenty dollars multiplied by five houses equals $100 per month or $1,200 per year. If my payments were to keep dropping by $20 per year my annual cash flow would be $6,000 larger in five years. And this doesn't take into account any rent increases!

This happy discovery about how adjustable rate mortgages work combined with a period of low inflation allowed me to modify my goal. Instead of buying five houses and waiting until I paid off the mortgages before I retired, I bought my five houses (plus a few others), prepaid on my mortgages every month, and semi-retired in my thirties.

By setting a goal and taking action, you'll be setting the stage for fortuitous discoveries with your own investments. It's okay if you don't know exactly how you'll reach your goal when you start. When I purchased my first investment house I had no idea how I would manage to buy the next one. But since I was looking, I did buy that house and then the next one. You can do it, too. Having a goal is the most important step in the right direction.

## If You Dislike Adjustable Rate Mortgages

You may not feel comfortable with adjustable rate mortgages. Does that mean this book isn't for you? Not at all. I acquired my houses using a mixture of fixed rate and adjustable rate mortgages. You may use only fixed rate loans if you prefer. Eventually you'll have to either pay them off or refinance them if you want your payments to disappear or become smaller. You may have to wait longer to retire or else have to pay refinancing fees before you can semi-retire, but fixed rate mortgages will get you where you want to go. The techniques in this book will still work well for you.

If you are intrigued by the idea of loan payments which become smaller, but you are concerned about interest rates going up, you should consider buying some properties with fixed loans and others with adjustable rate mortgages. Then you can use the extra cash flow from all of your properties to prepay your adjustable loans. This strategy will allow you to balance your risk. If rates go up, you'll only be affected on a couple of your properties. And if rates stay stable, you'll have some mortgage payments which will drop in a very satisfying way.

## Why Isn't Everyone Buying Real Estate?

I believe the average person can retire or at least semi-retire in less than ten years by investing in real estate. Maybe it won't be a luxurious retirement, but it will be enjoyable. Anybody with a reasonable amount of intelligence and the ability to get along with people can do very well in real estate.

Perhaps you are puzzled. If real estate investing is the perfect part-time self-employment opportunity, why isn't everyone buying houses? Surely it must be difficult or unpleasant to make money by owning rental properties.

## Compounding Interest

Before we go any further, I want to show you an example to demonstrate why most people do not become rich by investing in real estate. The problem is understanding the power of compounding interest. It took me years to fully comprehend how compounding interest can make a person rich, and why so few people take advantage of this power.

Let's suppose a woman offers you a job. This job will last for thirty-five days. She will pay you one of two ways. Either she will pay you $1,000 per day or she will pay you a penny the first day, two pennies the second day, four pennies the third day, and so forth. Every day you will be paid twice as much as the day before. Which method of payment would you choose?

If you are like most people you can recognize a trick question when you see one. You want to be paid by the second method, of course. But here's the tough question: how much more will the second method pay you?

It's easy to calculate your total pay if you choose the first payment option. Thirty-five days multiplied by $1,000 equals $35,000. Calculating the total pay for the second option is not as simple. Before you write down your pay for each of the thirty-five days and add it up, guess the second amount off the top of your head. Will it be twice as much as $35,000? Ten times as much? One hundred times as much?

The second method pays a grand total of $343,597,363.21. If you find this difficult to believe, get out a piece of paper and write down the numbers in a row, then add them up with your calculator. You probably substantially underestimated how much income the second option would generate.

You should also notice how slow the pay increases are in the beginning. If you were at a cocktail party during the fifth day of your job, you could tell someone that you earned sixteen cents that day.

But let's say the guy you are talking to accepted the same type of job but chose the first payment option. When he tells you he's making $1,000 a day, how are you going to feel? Not too clever. Probably you'll decide you selected the wrong payment plan. Without a solid understanding of how compounding interest can eventually make you rich, you might quit your job and get one like his.

Intellectually, you may understand that you will eventually do better financially than this man because your income is doubling every day while his remains stable, but that's hard to believe when he's out-earning and out-spending you in the beginning.

Getting rich requires some sacrifices up front. You look and feel poor because you are being frugal and saving while everyone else around you is buying fancy consumer items. It seems easier to chase after the high paying jobs rather than to plan for the future through investing, but a high paying job won't give you security. You can be downsized by a company with hardly any notice.

Of course it's easier to get ahead if you do have a high-paying job, but that won't necessarily make you financially independent in the long run. You must also save your money and invest it. Sure, your savings may not impress anybody when you start out, but at some point in time your investments will begin multiplying in quantities large enough to make your frugality seem worthwhile.

The first years are the hardest ones. Can you stick to your plan for four or five years, long enough to see how much progress you've made? Or will you be like many small real estate investors and jump ship after only two or three years? You should make at least a five year commitment to real estate if you want the chance to experience substantial financial rewards.

## Your Fellow Investor

It helps to have fellow investors to encourage you. My twin sister, Shelley, and her husband, Brandon, also adopted a five house goal. They began to buy rental houses. Much of their free time and a high percentage of Brandon's income were earmarked for their investment activities. Instead of buying new cars, furniture or clothes, they saved their money to buy houses.

When my twin sister reached the four year point in her investment career she would sometimes complain to me. "Is this really worth it? I'm so tired of being poor. All Brandon and I do is put our money and our time into our rentals. Will this really pay off someday?"

Since I was still a novice investor myself, I did my best to reassure her. The numbers made sense, and if we held tight we would all do well. We just had to be patient.

Less than two years later my sister was singing a different tune. She and her husband had a rental cash flow of over $18,000 per year. They only needed to buy one more property to reach their goal of five houses. After that purchase they could focus on paying off some of their fixed mortgages. They figured it would take two and a half years to pay off the first of their mortgages and then their cash flow would jump to almost twenty-five thousand dollars per year.

Did I still get calls from my sister? Of course, but she was happily planning what she and her husband would do with that soon-to-be-realized extra twenty-five thousand per year. Would Brandon quit his full time job and get a part-time job instead? Would they move back to Colorado once they weren't tied to Brandon's job in Texas anymore? Or would they postpone their semi-retirement another couple of years so they could pay off their personal home?

## Milt's Story

Milt has never liked debt. When he bought his personal residence he furnished it with items from the Salvation Army store and concentrated on paying down his mortgage with what he describes as a neurotic fixation. With the birth of his daughter he realized he needed to earn more money, but he didn't see any possibility of getting a lucrative job due to his lack of credentials.

Because of a sharp increase in the value of his home, though, Milt did have equity he could use as collateral for loans. He had never considered investing in real estate, but the appreciation on his home encouraged him to explore buying another property. His research convinced him that real estate was his best bet for achieving financial freedom.

For the first few years being a landlord seemed to involve a lot of work with very little reward. Milt invested the majority of his cash flow and a lot of his spare time into improving his three investment properties, adding such items as dishwashers and decks.

But when Milt reached his fifth year as a real estate investor, he started to see the payoff for all his hard work. Due to his past fix up work his maintenance costs were low on his properties. His spendable cash flow ranged up to $800 a month, a fabulous amount as far as Milt was concerned. He decided he liked being a landlord.

## How Many Houses Will You Need?

How many houses will you need to own to achieve your goals? It depends on how profitable rental real estate is where you live. You need to figure out how much income a good rental house will generate in a community nearby. Then you'll be able to figure out how many houses you will need to own so you can earn your target income. A blank worksheet is provided in Appendix A for you to use as you work through the rental numbers for your area. The bottom half of the worksheet is filled out with the numbers from the example we are about to do. You may want to make a copy of it so you can refer to it easily as you read through the example.

If you don't like math, you may not want to do these calculations. You may decide that owning three or five houses sounds fine to you, and you'll find out later if you need an extra property to meet your income goal. If you are this type of person, you can skim this next part, but you should still read the section later in this chapter which talks about estimating maintenance costs. When you are evaluating houses you could buy, comparing anticipated maintenance costs can help you choose the property you want to own.

## How Much Does a Three Bedroom House Cost?

You need to find out what a three bedroom, two bath house with approximately 1,300 square feet is selling for in a neighborhood within half an hour's drive of your home. If you live in a snowy state where garages are common, your sample property should also have a two car garage. Try to find houses which were built after 1980 if possible.

Since we're going to pretend that this target house is owned free and clear, you don't need to worry about mortgage rates or loan payments. But you will have to find out what the property taxes and insurance would be, plus how much this property would rent for in your area.

## Determining Property Tax and Insurance

When you do your research on property tax, remember that you may live in a state where investors are charged higher taxes than homeowners. You must always ask for and use the investor tax amount. The same is true for insurance, but in reverse. Usually a landlord policy is cheaper than a homeowner policy because it only covers liability and the structure, not the contents.

Look in the newspaper for ads describing properties which match your target house. Ask the listing agents for the addresses. A call to the tax assessor will provide you with the investor taxes for that property. Now call your insurance agent to get an approximate idea of what the insurance would cost.

# Rental Rates for Your Target Property

Next you need to determine what your rents would be. Look in the newspaper again and call on ads which describe properties similar to your target house. Ask real estate agents, professional property managers or other investors what rent amount they think is appropriate. Make sure you are getting rents for the same type of house as your sample house. A three bedroom house built in the fifties will not rent for the same amount as a three bedroom house built in the eighties. Get rents for houses comparable to your sample house.

When you have a monthly rent figure you believe is accurate, multiple it by 11.5 months instead of 12 months to get the yearly rent. Why? Because you will experience occasional vacancies. For this example we'll assume your average vacancy rate will be half a month per year. (If vacancy rates in your area are much higher according to local property managers or the newspaper reports, you should adjust this. Maybe one month's vacancy would be more accurate if your area is in a slump). Let's say the anticipated rent is $1,100 per month. Multiplying this by 11.5 months gives us $12,650 for the yearly rent.

# Projecting Maintenance Costs

Maintenance costs can be tricky to predict. You'll have to guesstimate what your average annual maintenance costs will be. Budget $250 for all the small stuff such as replacing heating elements in the oven, repairing broken gate latches or running 'For Rent' ads in the newspaper. Major expenditures such as new carpeting, a new roof, or repainting inside and out need to be amortized over a period of years to give you an anticipated average yearly cost. You will predict which of these costs will occur in the next ten years. A worksheet is provided in Appendix B for you to photocopy and complete.

For example, if you buy an eight-year-old frame house, you can count on repainting the exterior twice in the next ten years. The furnace probably will need to be replaced. The roof will most likely need a new layer of shingles, the hot water heater will die, and you'll have to repaint and recarpet the interior.

Let's add up the anticipated ten year costs assuming that you will be too busy or unwilling to do any of the work yourself.

| | |
|---|---|
| **Repainting exterior ($1,500 X 2)** | **$3,000** |
| **New furnace** | **$1,500** |
| **New roof** | **$3,000** |
| **New hot water heater** | **$450** |
| **Repaint interior** | **$1,200** |
| **New carpet** | **$2,000** |
| **New vinyl** | **$1,200** |
| **Total** | **$12,350** |

$12,350 divided by ten years gives you $1,235 each year for long-term maintenance items. Add the $250 for the annual small expenses. This gives you an average annual maintenance cost of $1,485.

Add your taxes and insurance to get your total annual costs. Let's say taxes would be $1,100 and insurance $360 for the sample house. So the total annual costs would be $2,945. (In general older houses will have higher average annual maintenance costs, but will have better rent to property value ratios compared to newer houses.)

# How Much Cash Flow Per House?

Next you need to subtract your total average annual costs from the anticipated rent. Using the numbers from this example we have $12,650 in rent and $2,945 for the average yearly out-of-pocket expense. When you subtract the expense amount from the rent you get $9,705. This is the spendable cash flow you would receive each year if you owned the house free and clear today.

Remember that the cash flow number you calculate for your sample house will not be the same as in this example unless your area magically has the same type of rents and anticipated costs. You must use the information you collected about your local rental market and repair cost to determine an annual cash flow for a 1,300 square foot house in a community near you.

## How Many Houses Do You Want to Own?

Knowing how much income one house will produce is the first step. The next question to answer is how many houses you will need to own to earn your target income. This step is very simple. Divide the annual income you want by the cash flow produced by your sample rental house and you'll find out how many houses you need to acquire.

For this example let's assume your annual income goal is $50,000. Since our sample rental house generates a $9,705 annual cash flow, we'll divide $50,000, your income goal, by $9,705, the cash flow your target house would generate each year. This gives us 5.15.

Since it's difficult to buy .15 of a house, you have a small problem. The easy answer is to settle for five houses. Five houses producing $9,705 per year equals a $48,525 annual income. This may be close enough to your income goal to satisfy you. Or you could decide to buy six houses. That would produce an annual income of $58,230.

## If You Want to Be Exact

If you want to have an exact goal, you can take these numbers one step further. For our example a $130,000 house owned free and clear will generate $9,705 per year in cash flow after all expenses. You want to know how much cash flow is generated by each thousand you have invested. $130,000 is $1,000 multiplied by 130. So you divide the cash flow of $9,705 by 130 and get $74.65. This means that for every $1,000 your properties are worth, you'll receive $74.65 in cash flow each year.

We can use this number to calculate the total amount your target houses must be worth to generate your income goal of $50,000. Divide $50,000 by $74.65. This gives you 670. This is how many thousands of dollars worth of houses you'll need to own to generate your target income. For this example you would want to own houses worth a total of $670,000.

| | |
|---|---|
| 130,000/1,000 | 130 |
| $9,0705/130 | $74.65 |
| $50,000/$74.65 | 670 |
| 670 X $1,000 | $670,000 |

This means you could decide to own four houses worth $130,000 for a total of $520,000 plus one more house worth $150,000 for a grand total of $670,000. Or else you could own four houses worth $167,500 each. Another option would be to own ten houses or condominiums worth $67,000 apiece. The combinations are endless. Your goal is to acquire properties worth a total of $670,000, pay them off, and then enjoy your $50,000 annual income. (Use the worksheet in Appendix C to calculate the cash flow per $1,000 invested based on your sample property.)

# Different Rental Ratios for Different Houses

You should realize that the rent-to-property value ratio is not the same in all price ranges. The amount of cash flow generated by each thousand dollars worth of house you own will vary depending on the price point of that house. In our example we calculated the cash flow on a starter house worth $130,000. If you buy a house worth substantially more than $130,000, for example $230,000, you will get less rent for each dollar you have invested. Properties in the upper price ranges for any given area rent for less compared to their market value than do lower priced houses. (Remember, if starter houses in your area cost $230,000, then the rent ratio will be less for mid-priced houses, which in your area may cost $415,000.)

For example, in Westminster, Colorado, houses which sold for $100,000 in 1998 rented for $995, a 99.5% ratio of monthly rent-to-property value. Houses which sold for $130,000 rented for $1,105, or an 85% ratio. Houses which sold for $200,000 rented for $1,575 per month, or a 79% ratio.

You may be thinking, "Aha! I'll only buy properties at the low end of the market since they are more profitable." This is true, but lower cost properties come with disadvantages of their own. See Chapter 4, Selecting Properties, for an in-depth look at which properties you may want to own and why. The rent-to-property value ratio is only one factor to consider when you choose properties.

## How Long Will It Take You?

Now that you have a target net worth of properties you want to own, the next question to answer is how long it will take you to acquire these properties and pay them off. We'll assume for this example that you are shooting for full retirement with the understanding that you can decide to semi-retire anywhere along the way.

For this step you'll need to either use your financial calculator or else find someone else who has one and knows how to use it. Most real estate agents own a financial calculator and can help you. I'll tell you how to use a Texas Instrument financial calculator as we go through this example since that's what I own. Stores such as Target sell this calculator for under twenty dollars.

Here are the numbers you'll need before you can predict when you'll be financially independent.

**a) What is the combined target value of the houses you plan to buy? (your net worth goal)**
**b) What is the value of your current assets available to invest in real estate (or already invested in real estate)?**
**c) How much money can you save for investing each year out of your regular income?**
**d) How many years are you willing to wait to reach your goal?**

With these four numbers you can compute the missing fifth number which is the rate of return you will need to earn on an annual basis in order to reach your goal. If the required rate of return is a reasonable number, one you know you can earn, fine. Full steam ahead. If it's too high, a rate you don't think is possible, you'll have to adjust your goal or your timetable. If the rate is ridiculously low, you may be able to increase your goal or get there faster than you thought you could.

Let's say you have a goal of owning properties worth $670,0000. This is your net worth goal. You have $20,000 either available in savings to invest in real estate or you have already invested that same $20,000 in one or more rental properties. You are saving $3,000 per year from your regular income. You are willing to wait twelve years before you retire.

## Using Your Texas Instrument Calculator

Turn on your calculator by pressing the AC/ON button. To put your calculator into the correct FIN mode, press the CE/C button and then the button marked 2nd.

Now enter 670,000, your net worth goal, and press the FV, future value, button.

Enter 20,000, your current assets available for real estate investment, and hit the PV, present value, button.

Enter 3,000, your annual savings, then press the -/+ key to make this number negative (this number must be negative to do the calculation correctly). Now press the PMT, payment, button.

Enter 12 for the number of years before you want to retire and press the N, number of years, button.

Finally, press the CPT, compute, button and the % i, annual rate of interest or return, button. The calculator will calculate the annual interest rate you need to earn based on the numbers you entered.

The calculator will tell you that you'll have to earn a 29.66% rate of return on your invested money each year for the next twelve years to reach your retirement goal of $670,000 assuming that you start with $20,000 and add $3,000 per year. While this rate of return is possible, you'll either have to be in an appreciating market or create forced appreciation by fixing up dumpy properties to get a rate of return this high.

If you aren't willing to count on a quickly appreciating market and you are not the fixer upper type of person, you have some other options. You can change a few of your figures. You may be willing to increase the amount you currently have to invest by selling your boat or perhaps your record collection and investing the proceeds into real estate. Increasing your initial investment can be very powerful. That money will have many years to compound in value.

If getting more money to invest at the beginning is not possible then you may decide you are willing to wait fifteen years to retire instead of twelve years. This one change drops the annual interest rate you need to receive down to 22.28%. This would be much easier to earn than 29.66%.

But let's say you really want to retire in twelve years. You could get a second job that pays you $7,000 after taxes. This would give you $10,000 to invest each year instead of $3,000. This would reduce the annual interest rate you need to earn down to 22.08%.

Possibly none of these compromises appeals to you or is possible. The last figure you can change is your net worth goal. If you are willing to retire with a net worth of $453,661 invested in real estate instead of $670,000, you would need to earn only a 25% annual rate of return. Perhaps you are counting on a pension or IRA to start paying out at the same time you retire. Those payments could make up the difference in your income. Or maybe you could do a little part-time work after you retire.

The options become endless when you start to change more than one element at a time. The bottom line is that it is very possible for most of us to fully retire in less than twenty years. And semi-retirement can be much sooner.

## The Real World

The above example is simplified. In the real world while you are saving up your extra cash flow for the down payment on the next house, you won't get a great rate of return on that money. If you are saving your money in a money market fund, you may receive only 6% instead of the 20-30% you can receive once you buy your next house. This period of time when your money earns a smaller rate of return will slow down your progress to your goal.

In addition our example assumes that you won't lose any of your equity through the inevitable costs of selling one or more of your properties if you decide to exchange them into different properties. Money spent on commissions, closing costs, and exchange fees will no longer be compounding in your favor. Once spent, it will be gone. This is why you should try to avoid selling properties if possible.

Despite these real world problems, this method of planning the future will give you a rough idea of how long it will take you to reach your goal. Since life is full of surprises, things will happen which will both help and hinder you on your journey. That's okay. Adjust to your changing circumstances and keep on taking action to achieve your goal. If you are persistent you will reach it, probably sooner than you anticipated.

# Chapter Two

# Rate of Return on Rental Real Estate

To achieve your financial goals within a particular time frame, you'll need to earn a minimum rate of return on your real estate investments. To find out if you are on track toward reaching your goal, you'll need to know what rate of return you are receiving.

You will also want to use projected rates of return to compare properties. If you find two houses you would like to buy, but you can only afford to purchase one, projecting their anticipated rates of return will allow you to compare them against each other.

You may also want to compare potential rates of return on real estate investments against the rates of return you think you could earn on other types of investments. Would real estate be a better investment than buying stocks or bonds or an interest in your brother's new computer software company?

Your predictions, though, are exactly that, predictions. When you calculate the potential rates of return, you will be doing a lot of guesswork. Your predictions may or may not turn out to be accurate. While the information in this chapter is valuable, some people frankly won't care to learn how to calculate rates of return. They know they love real estate and that's where they want to invest their money. They also know that if they buy property and pay off the mortgages, they will eventually be able to retire and live their dream lives.

If you want to skip this chapter and dive right into selecting properties and handling tenants, that's fine. Whether or not you do the rate of return numbers, your properties will still appreciate, you'll save money on your taxes due to depreciation, your mortgages will gradually be paid off, and you'll receive cash flow each month. You can profit handsomely by investing in real estate even if you never learn how to calculate your annual rates of return.

## Calculating Your Rate of Return

Calculating the rate of return on your real estate investments is more complicated than with stocks or certificates of deposit. Before you invest in a certificate of deposit you know what interest rate you'll be paid. Rates of return on stocks can be calculated by adding up any dividends you receive plus the amount of appreciation (or depreciation) you experience in the stocks' values in a one year period of time. These two numbers combined are divided by the amount of money you had invested in the stocks to give you the annual rate of return you received on your investment.

To determine your rate of return on real estate investments you must add together four types of return. You'll receive appreciation (or depreciation) in the value of your properties, cash flow, principal paydown on your mortgages, plus federal and state income tax savings. In order to determine your total annual rate of return, you'll have to figure out how much you made in each of these four areas.

# Appreciation

Appreciation is where you can make the most money the quickest. If you are fortunate enough to buy in an appreciating market, your gains can add up to impressive numbers in just a few years. Suppose that you own a house worth $120,000. If it goes up 4% in value next year, that's a gain of $4,800. If your house, now worth $124,800, goes up 4% again the following year, you'll make an additional $4,992. By adding these gains together, your house would increase in value by almost $10,000 in just two years.

Appreciation like this is wonderful when you own a house free and clear, but it becomes even more amazing when you use leverage to increase your rate of return. Leverage is when you combine your money with someone else's money to make investments.

## The Amazing Power of Leverage

For example, let's say you buy two houses. Each house costs $100,000. You buy the first one using all cash and the second one by putting $20,000 down and getting an $80,000 mortgage. What happens if the real estate market appreciates 3% the next year? What will be your rate of return from appreciation on each of these houses?

You invested $100,000 cash in the first house and at the end of the year it is worth $103,000. When you divide the $3,000 gain by the $100,000 you have invested, you get a 3% rate of return.

But you invested only $20,000 of your own money in the second house. It also went up in value $3,000. When you divide the $3,000 gain by the $20,000 invested, you get a 15% rate of return. By using leverage you have multiplied your rate of return on your invested money by five. Clearly, you will reach your goal much faster if you use the power of leverage.

Let's suppose you really leverage your money. What would your rate of return be if you bought a $100,000 house with no money down and the house appreciated $3,000 in one year? You couldn't even calculate your rate of return due to appreciation. A $3,000 gain divided by zero is infinity!

# Getting Into Trouble

This is how a lot of investors get into trouble. Yes, leveraging your money is a smart thing to do, but within prudent limits. Why? Because although you will be a fantastic success in an appreciating market, you may lose everything in a depreciating market.

Let's say you buy a $100,000 house with no money down, and the market depreciates by 3%. Instead of having an infinite gain, you have an infinite loss. If instead you had $20,000 invested in the house, your loss on your invested money would be reduced to 15%. And if you owned the house free and clear, you would lose only 3% of your invested money.

So while you can use leverage to increase your rate of return dramatically in the good years, it will also magnify your losses in the down years. The more equity you have the less dramatic the results.

Does this mean you should avoid leverage? Not at all. Using leverage is essential if you want to reach your goals within a short period of time. The key is to find a good balancing point between using leverage and controlling your risk.

I feel that a 20% equity position will allow you to weather the temporary downswings so you can enjoy the recoveries which follow. Having equity in a rental property permits you to comfortably handle the market's downswings because more equity equals smaller loan payments. And a smaller loan payment gives you more room to drop rents without ending up with a negative cash flow.

I believe that you will experience appreciation if you hold your properties for at least seven years. Even though the market falls occasionally, historically it has consistently gone up. Just think about what your parents paid for their house. My parents built a four bedroom, three bath, two car garage home on two and a half acres in the early sixties for less than $33,000. That house is worth almost $300,000 today.

# The Future of Appreciation

Just because real estate has appreciated in the past does not automatically mean it will continue to appreciate in the future. So why am I confident it will rise in value?

Real estate will continue to appreciate for two reasons. The first is inflation. Even at the low current inflation rates of 1-3%, property prices will double every twenty to thirty years. For example, let's say I buy a rental house today which costs $130,000. By the time my nephew, Spencer, who is eleven years old, grows up and marries, this house will probably cost him $250,000.

The second reason I believe the real estate market will continue to appreciate is because of the population demographics of the United States. In 1970 the population of this country was 203,000,000. In 1980 and 1990, it had increased to 227,000,000 and 249,000,000 respectively. By the year 2010, it is predicted to be 297,000,000.

Where are all these people going to live? More houses and apartments and condominiums will be built, of course. But the locations of these new homes may not be as desirable as the locations of houses built before the turn of the century.

For example, a new business park is being built between the cities of Boulder and Denver. Tens of thousands of new jobs are being created in a relatively small area. The employees who take these jobs will prefer to live in homes which are close to work so they can have short commutes.

As traffic congestion continues to worsen in the Denver area, an increasing premium will be put on properties which are conveniently located close to this business park. Already property values in this sub-area are rising faster than in other comparable neighborhoods in the Denver metro area. I own four and a half houses here, and I am confident that I will continue to receive an attractive rate of appreciation for years to come.

## Cash Flow

The second rate of return in real estate comes from cash flow. If you have 20% equity in a property, you should be able to rent the property for enough money to cover the mortgage and expenses with some cash flow left over. If you want to have fun being a property owner it's important to be paid each month for your property management duties. If the properties you are considering for purchase will not produce a comfortable cash flow with a 20% equity investment, then you are either looking at the wrong properties or the properties are in a bad rental area.

A bad rental area may be a desirable place for homeowners to live, but because rents are too low compared to property values, it will be a bad area to own rental property. I go into more detail about which properties will provide an acceptable rent-to-property value ratio in Chapter Four, Selecting Properties.

## Principal Paydown

The third rate of return you'll receive in real estate is principal paydown. Even if your properties never rise in value you will eventually pay off the mortgages. In the beginning years only a small portion of your payments will go toward principal, but the proportion of your payments which go to principal will increase at an ever faster rate as the years go by.

Principal paydown is an invisible rate of return. If you ask someone to tell you the four ways to make money in real estate, this is usually the last one they'll mention. In the past I've had students in my real estate investment classes tell me that principal paydown doesn't really count since you can't get to it without selling. After all, maybe the market will collapse and all your equity will disappear.

But principal paydown is real. When you go to the bank to get a loan, they will subtract your current mortgage balance from your property's current value when they calculate its contribution to your net worth. By paying down your loan balance, you are increasing your net worth. This makes you a stronger borrower in the bank's eyes. You can also borrow against your increased equity to pull out money to put down on another property. Banks obviously do not think your increased equity is imaginary if they are willing to use it as collateral.

Finally, at the end of your loan term, you will have paid off your mortgage. Eliminating the mortgage payment is a very real benefit! More than any other rate of return you can count on principal paydown to someday give you large monthly cash flows.

## Depreciation

The last rate of return is the income tax savings you'll realize each year from owning real estate. Following the tax laws in this country, the Internal Revenue Service acts as if residential rental property is depreciating, that is losing value. Of course, if you have purchased a desirable property and are maintaining it, it is actually going to increase in value over time. Despite this fact the Internal Revenue Service lets you shield some of your income through depreciation.

To calculate how much depreciation you can claim on each house, you must first determine what proportion of its value comes from the improvements and what proportion of its value is in the land. Why? Because although the Internal Revenue Service acts as if your houses are falling down over time, they realize that the land will still be there. The land will maintain its value and therefore cannot be depreciated.

Before you can depreciate a house, you need to determine its worth separate from the land beneath it. A simple way to do this is to use the tax assessor's valuation. Most assessors will give a value to the land, let's say $5,000. Then they'll assign a value to the improvements, let's say $20,000. According to the assessor, the total value is the combination of these two figures, $25,000.

When you divide the improvement value of $20,000 by the total value of $25,000, you find that the improvements equal 80% of the total property value. If you paid $120,000 for this house (ignoring some closing costs which can also be depreciated), you multiply this price by 80%. $120,000 multiplied by 80% is $96,000. This is the value you can claim for the improvements.

The Internal Revenue Service assigns a lifetime to all capital items. Houses are currently supposed to last 27.5 years. In our example we divide the value of the improvements, $96,000, by 27.5 years. This produces an annual depreciation loss of $3,491. Since you are "losing" value in your investment, the Internal Revenue Service will let you deduct this loss against your income as long as you qualify as an active investor. (Per Internal Revenue Publication 527, you are an active investor if you make management decisions such as "approving new tenants, deciding on rental terms, approving expenditures and similar decisions.")

While depreciation is a wonderful way to reduce your current tax burden, there are restrictions. For most investors the total amount of depreciation you can claim for all your properties combined is limited to $25,000 per year. One exception to this limit is when you have more than $25,000 in passive income (according to Internal Revenue Service definitions, cash flow from real estate investments is considered passive income).

The $25,000 depreciation deduction limit applies only when you take passive losses from real estate against active income such as the money you earn working at a job, not when you apply it to income from your real estate investments. If your passive income from real estate exceeds $25,000, you may be able to take a larger amount of depreciation losses.

On the negative side, you won't be allowed to deduct up to the full $25,000 if you have a high adjusted income. If your adjusted income is over $100,000 per year, your right to take the full depreciation deduction begins to be phased out. If you earn over $150,000 in adjusted income, you will not be allowed to take any depreciation at all. You should talk to your accountant to see how the depreciation limits apply to you.

## To Depreciate or Not to Depreciate

Even if you don't like the idea of depreciating your properties, you still have to do it. Sometimes I'll meet people who tell me their accountant told them they don't have to depreciate their rental properties. But according to the tax experts I've consulted, and Publication 527, if you don't depreciate your properties and later sell them, the Internal Revenue Service will calculate your taxes as if you HAD depreciated the properties. If you didn't depreciate your properties, too bad!

By not depreciating you will lose the tax savings while you own the property and you will have to pay the taxes when you sell. Your only option will be to amend your tax returns for the previous three years so you can depreciate your properties on those returns (three years is the limit for amending past returns). If you own rental properties and you haven't been depreciating them, you may want to ask your accountant if the numbers make it worthwhile for you to amend your most recent returns.

Depreciation is a wonderful tax shelter for the small investor. Whatever money you can save from the tax man today can be invested to get you to your goal that much sooner. While it's true that you will owe taxes on any gain you realize as an investor, these gains are only taxable when you sell. Instead of selling and taking the proceeds, you can do 1031 tax deferred exchanges (see Chapter Eleven, 1031 Tax Deferred Exchanges).

Or you can keep your properties until you die. At the time of your death the value of all your real estate becomes its basis, or its official cost according to the Internal Revenue Service. So if you buy a house for $100,000 and depreciate it down to $50,000, you would owe deferred taxes on the difference when and if you sell the house.

But if instead you die and leave the property to your heirs, the $50,000 basis will jump up to current market value, let's say $125,000. If the total value of your estate is below federal estate limits, your heirs won't owe any estate taxes. If they sell your properties for the value the properties had at the time of your death, your heirs won't owe any capital gains tax either. By dying, you have done more than just defer taxes - you have eliminated them!

Of course you should consult an estate attorney when you make your estate decisions. Besides the fact that I am not an attorney, the tax laws are constantly changing. In addition your individual circumstances will strongly influence your estate planning decisions. But this is one of the smoothest ways to avoid taxes that I've discovered.

# Calculating Rates of Return

Rate of return calculations are done using five numbers. For any given year you will need to determine how much money you had invested in a property, the cash flow you received that year after subtracting expenses, how much your loan balance decreased (principal paydown), how much your property appreciated (or depreciated), and how much you saved on federal and state income taxes.

Almost all of this information has to be collected and put on your property tax return form, the Schedule E. Since you have to do the numbers for Uncle Sam, you may as well do one more step and calculate how fast your net worth is increasing.

To get an accurate number for your annual rate of return, you need to put the correct numbers into the formulas I'm about to give you. The definitions for each number you need will be explained.

## Amount Invested

This number changes every year. The first year you need to add up the down payment, closing costs, and any expenditures during the year for improvements such as a deck or finished basement (do not include maintenance or advertising costs). This is the money out-of-pocket you had to pay for the property plus any capital improvements.

The second year you start with the first year's figure, but you add to it. Your loan balance is lower because you paid it down a bit the prior year, and that principal paydown is now equity tied up in your property. The appreciation you received the previous year is also tied up as equity in your house.

You must take the first year's amount invested and increase it by adding last year's principal paydown amount and the appreciation amount. Each succeeding year, increase your total amount invested by adding the paydown and appreciation amounts for the previous year.

You should also add the cost of any improvements, not repairs, that you make to the property. An improvement is a large expenditure which cannot be written off in the year you pay for it, but instead has to be depreciated. An improvement would be something such as finishing a basement, adding a bath or deck, or getting a new furnace or roof.

If you refinance your property, you should reduce the figure for the amount invested by subtracting the amount of money you pull out of the property. For example, if you have $50,000 invested, and you refinance and take out $30,000 cash, you've reduced the amount of money you have invested in this property. Instead of $50,000 you now have $20,000 invested.

Don't get the amount invested confused with your equity. The amount invested is bigger than your equity because it includes money you'll never see again such as closing costs. That $20,000 invested will be bigger than your equity unless you bought a property without incurring any closing costs.

To keep your figures 100% accurate when you refinance, you will also need to allocate the cost of the refinancing to a particular property. You could add your refinancing closing costs to the amount invested in the property you refinanced or if you refinanced to buy another property, you could add the refinancing cost to the amount invested for the new property. I prefer to put the refinancing costs toward the new house since I regard it as the price I had to pay to get the down payment.

## Cash Flow

Add up your rent received for the year and subtract maintenance costs, attorney or accounting fees, any eviction fees, and your mortgage payments. If taxes or insurance are not included in the mortgage payments, but are paid separately, subtract those costs as well.

## Principal Paydown

This is an easy number because each January your mortgage company will tell you how much you paid down your mortgage since the last year. The principal paid figure will include the principal you were required to pay each month plus any principal you prepaid.

# Appreciation

What is your house worth today compared to the same time last year? You may have a good feeling for the market value, or you can ask your real estate agent to run comps (comparison sales) for other properties which recently sold. (Instead of appreciation, you may experience depreciation some years if real estate values go down.)

There is no way to determine the exact amount of appreciation without selling the house, so use your best guess. I tend to err on the conservative side, that is I'll say $3,000 instead of $4,000. I can always adjust upward in future years if necessary.

# Tax Savings

You will save on your taxes because of depreciation. If you own a house where the improvements excluding the land are worth $82,500, you are losing $3,000 per year according to the tax laws of this country. The value of this deduction depends on your tax bracket. What is your combined local, state and federal tax bracket? If your combined income tax rate is 20%, then multiply $3,000 by 20%. You will save $600 in the taxes you won't owe that year.

# Calculating Your Total Rate of Return

Now that you have your five numbers, what do you do with them? You have two options. Take numbers two through five and add them together, then divide them by the first number. This is your total rate of return for the past year. If you want to see exactly how your rate of return is broken down by category, you should divide numbers two through five individually by the first number. Then add these four partial rates of return together to get your total rate of return for the year.

## Realistic Rates of Return

What is a realistic rate of return to aim for when you buy rental properties? This varies depending on how much money you have invested in a property, and this depends on how long you've owned the property. Your leverage is usually highest during the first few years so this is when you'll probably see your highest rates of return. Since your rate of return will decrease over time due to your increasing equity and therefore decreasing leverage, you should aim for a first year return of at least 20% per year. If you can get 25% or 30%, that would be preferable.

If you've owned a property for a number of years, your rate of return on your invested money may go down to 15% or lower. If you've already purchased all the properties you need for your goal, you may not care about a falling rate of return. All you want to do at this point is pay off your mortgages and retire.

But if you still need to acquire other properties, you may want to pull some of your invested money out by getting a second mortgage or by using a 1031 tax deferred exchange to switch your equity from one house into down payments on two or more houses. This will increase your leverage and help you increase your rates of return to above 20% again.

## Rate of Return Example

To show you a sample rate of return you can expect as an average investor, we're going to look at the numbers for a house I own in Colorado. A blank worksheet is provided in Appendix D for you to copy and use when you calculate the rate of return for a property you already own or to predict the rate of return for a property you are considering buying.

I bought this particular property in the late fall of 1994, but the figures in this example are based on my first full year of ownership in 1995. The house was purchased for $124,500 with 20% down with closing costs of $2,155. I experienced two weeks of vacancy and had expenses which equalled $7,506. My loan balance was reduced by $2,022 and I estimated my appreciation to be $2,000 for that year. I was able to write off $4,075 as a depreciation expense against my income.

| | |
|---|---|
| **Purchase price** | **$124,500** |
| **New loan** | **$99,600** |
| **Down payment (purchase price - new loan)** | **$24,900** |
| **Closing costs** | **$2,155** |
| **Cash invested (closing costs + down payment)** | **$27,055** |
| **Income Received (11 1/2 months rent of $1,135)** | **$13,052** |

**Expenses**

| | | |
|---|---|---|
| | **Taxes** | **$983** |
| | **Interest** | **$5,925** |
| | **Insurance** | **$309** |
| **Misc.** | **Aeration and sprinkler system maint.** | **$50** |
| | **Landscape plants** | **$60** |
| | **2 weeks electricity, new burner, etc.** | **$92** |
| | **Rental ad in The Denver Post** | **$60** |
| | **Gate repair - parts** | **$27** |
| | **Total miscellaneous expenses** | **$289** |

| | |
|---|---|
| **Total Expenses** | **$7,506** |

**Cash flow**

| | |
|---|---|
| **(Income - expenses - principal paydown)** | **$3,524** |
| **Principal Paydown** | **$2,022** |
| **Appreciation** | **$2,000** |
| **Depreciation ($112,062 value of improvements divided by 27.5 years)** | **$4,075** |

The total rate of return is the combination of the four rates of return earned by real estate. The rates of return for principal paydown, cash flow, appreciation, and depreciation are calculated and then added together.

The cash flow rate of return is the cash flow, $3,524, divided by the total amount invested, $27,055. The rate of return from cash flow in 1995 was 13%.

I followed the same process to determine the rates of return for principal paydown and appreciation. The rate of return from principal paydown was 7.47% ($2,022 divided by $27,055) and appreciation was 7.39% ($2,000 divided by $27,055).

The rate of return from tax savings depended on my federal tax bracket. Assuming that the depreciation savings applied across two income tax brackets (where some income is taxed at one rate with the rest at a lower rate) I think I saved an average of 15% based on federal taxes plus 5% for the state of Colorado, or a total of 20%. $4,075 multiplied by 20% gave me a tax savings of $815. Divided by the total amount invested, $27,055, the rate of return from depreciation was 3%.

Added together these four rates of return gave me a total rate of return of 30.86%. This means the property generated 30.86% on the amount invested in it. In other words the $27,055 I had invested in this property increased by 30.86% in one year.

| | |
|---|---|
| **Cash flow** | **13.00%** |
| **Principal paydown** | **7.47%** |
| **Appeciation** | **7.39%** |
| **Depreciation** | **3.00%** |
| **Total Rate of Return** | **30.86%** |

# A 30% Rate of Return Compounded

To understand what a good rate of return 30% is, let's pretend we have $100,000 invested. If we receive a 30% rate of return for five years in a row, our original investment will become $371,293.

Let's say we keep our money invested for another two years. Continuing with an annual rate of return of 30% our investment would increase in value to $627,485. And if at the end of this seven year period our investment produced a cash flow of only 8% on our invested money, we would receive an income of $50,200 per year.

Of course, coming up with the initial $100,000 takes a number of years for most people. They don't have $100,000 to invest all at once. Plus it's hard to maintain a consistent annual rate of return of 30%. You won't be getting that rate of return on the cash flow and tax savings. In real life, you'll have to save that money up for your next down payment in a low interest bearing account such as a savings account or money market fund.

The reason I played this "what if" game was to illustrate again the incredible power of compounding interest. Compounding interest will make you rich if you have patience and persistence.

## Where to Save Your Money

Where should you save your cash flow and tax savings while you're accumulating enough money for your next down payment? One of the best places is in your own home. If you prepay on your mortgage, you'll save the 7-9% interest you would otherwise be paying. When you have saved enough to make a down payment on a good rental property, it's very easy to pull that money out using a home equity line of credit. To save up for the next house you will pay off the line of credit.

If you suspect, however, that your spouse may become attached to the new, lower mortgage on your own home and will refuse to pull out any of the increased equity, you may want to save your money in an account earmarked for investment purposes. In this case, your best choice is a money market fund at a bank. Your rate of return may not be as high and it will be taxable, but at least you'll be able to use the money to buy a rental property.

Another downside to putting money into a liquid money market account is how easy it is to pull it out. You may be tempted to spend it on short-term consumer items. When the money is tied up in your personal home, it takes a little bit more effort to get at it. Review your financial goals before you succumb to temptation. Hopefully you'll have plenty of money to spend in just a few more years.

## Decreasing Rate of Return

As I mentioned before, each year you own a property the total amount you have invested in it will increase because of the equity build-up from loan paydown plus accumulated appreciation. Each year when you calculate your rates of return, you'll be dividing your four rates of return by a bigger amount invested. When you divide by a bigger amount invested, you get a smaller rate of return. So your rate of return will usually decrease each year.

As an illustration let's look at the numbers from my property again. Let's say that all my numbers on this property stayed the same for 1996 as they were in 1995. Appreciation was $2,000 again. The principal paydown stayed at $2,022 (normally principal paydown goes up each year as you pay down a loan, but since I have an adjustable loan on this property anything can happen). My cash flow was $3,524 again and I saved another $815 on taxes. Everything stayed the same except for the total amount invested.

The total amount invested MUST have changed because I had more equity tied up in the property. For 1995 the total amount invested was $27,055. To get the total amount invested for 1996 we add 1995's principal paydown, $2,022, and the appreciation, $2,000, to the previous year's amount invested. The new total amount invested for 1996 was $31,077. If all the other numbers stayed constant, what would the total rate of return have been in 1996?

| | |
|---|---|
| **Principal paydown ($2,022/$31,077)** | **6.50%** |
| **Cash flow ($3,524/$31,077)** | **11.34%** |
| **Appreciation ($2,000/$31,077)** | **6.44%** |
| **Depreciation ($815/$31,077)** | **2.62%** |
| **Total Rate of Return** | **26.90%** |

Instead of a 30.6% combined rate of return, I would have received a 26.9% combined rate of return on my invested money. If these rate of return numbers stayed constant except for the total amount invested for another three years, my annual rate of return would drop to just under 20% by the end of year five.

There is one bright point to this tendency for rates of return to drop as the invested money in a property increases. The speed with which the rate of return decreases becomes slower each year. Between year one and year two my rate of return for our example drops by 3.08%. Between years four and five it drops by only 1.59%.

Though rates of return decrease as your leverage in a property decreases, there are some compensating factors. In the real world your principal paydown amount will probably increase every year instead of holding constant. Cash flow will rise faster than expenses, especially if you are prepaying on an adjustable loan so your mortgage payments decrease. Even if appreciation stays at a constant percentage, say 3%, your appreciation amount will increase each year because 3% of $150,000 is more than 3% of $130,000. Only your tax savings which is based on depreciating your property at its original purchase price will stay constant assuming you remain in the same tax bracket.

# Increasing Your Rate of Return

You can increase the rate of return on a property you have owned for a while by using one of two methods. First, you can refinance your property with a new first mortgage or add a second mortgage. Either way you are drawing money out to invest someplace else. Since you now have less money invested in the first property, you've increased your leverage and therefore your potential rate of return.

The second method is to sell your first property and 1031 tax defer exchange your equity into a more expensive property or into two or more properties with a combined value which is greater than the value of the property you've sold. For more information on 1031 tax deferred exchanges, see Chapter Eleven, 1031 Tax Deferred Exchanges.

No matter which method you decide to use to increase your rate of return, you'll lose some of your money in transaction costs. You'll either pay loan origination fees and title insurance payments for a new mortgage, or you'll have to pay real estate commissions, closing costs and exchange fees if you do a 1031 tax deferred exchange. Because of these costs, you shouldn't refinance or exchange until your current rate of return gets so low that it makes financial sense to restructure your investment.

# When to Restructure Your Investments

When do you reach this restructuring point? There is no hard and fast rule, but keep this guideline in mind. Depending on how soon you want to have a certain net worth and how much money you have to start with, you should calculate a bottom limit rate of return that will allow you to retire within a time frame that's agreeable to you. If your rate of return falls beneath this bottom limit, you'll need to restructure your investments in order to retire when you want.

Let's say you have a goal of $627,485 in equity in ten years and you have $100,000 to start with now. To reach your goal you use your financial calculator and determine that you need to get a yearly return of 20.16%. Averaging out your rates of return for different years, you know you can do better than that in the early years of owning a property which compensates for dropping below that rate later. So you decide 15% is your bottom line, a rate of return you insist on getting. If you reach that, it's time to restructure.

Personally, I like to look at how much five year certificates of deposit are paying. If they are paying 5%, then the bottom line rate of return I want to receive on my rentals is 15%. I figure I should get paid at least 10% more if I have to manage properties instead of loaning my money to a bank. I want to be paid for my time spent showing houses, cleaning them up, and keeping track of the paperwork.

If you abhor the idea of tracking your rates of return (too hard! you want to get rich, but you hate math), you can simply restructure whenever you can afford to do so. If investor loans require 20% down, wait until you have 40% equity in one property, then exchange your equity into two similarly priced properties (or refinance out the down payment for the second property), using additional savings to pay for the transaction costs.

## Ignoring Rates of Return

Once you have acquired your target number of rental properties, you may no longer care very much about your rates of return. If you have enough properties so when you pay off the mortgages the properties will generate sufficient income after taxes for you to live on, you will no longer be at the accumulation stage. Growth rates will no longer concern you.

You'll be at the plateau stage where your biggest concern will be having your rents appreciate as fast as inflation so your buying power stays constant. Perhaps you'll exchange into newer properties to keep your time spent making house repairs to a minimum, but at a certain point, your properties will require very little attention from you beyond basic property management.

This is the point where you can turn your energies to other interests and no longer worry about making a living. If you want to travel or do volunteer work or spend years learning how to weave rugs, you'll have the freedom to do so. It may be hard to stop focusing on making your money grow, but you should remind yourself why you wanted that money in the first place. Don't let getting rich in a monetary sense blind you to all the other riches that life has to offer.

# Chapter Three

# Down Payments

To invest in real estate you usually need to put down a substantial amount of cash. While a surprising number of people have a chunk of money to invest, this chapter is targeted toward those who aren't sure how they will come up with their down payments.

Books have been written about how to buy real estate with no money down. It is possible though it usually involves using somebody's money, even if it's not actually your money. Twice I have borrowed my down payment for a house from my mother, and another time I purchased a house in foreclosure using cash my parents raised in less than eight hours.

I know someone who borrowed from a number of friends in order to accumulate down payments and closing costs, though he did pledge the equity in his house as collateral. My sister and brother-in-law have traded fix up labor in exchange for a fifty percent ownership in two properties.

Down payments can be as little as nothing down even if you are not a veteran of the United States military (veterans can get zero down VA loans). Specialty loans where someone pledges collateral are available with zero down for anyone who qualifies, veteran or not. For example, World Savings and Washington Mutual both offer 100% loan-to-value loans (see Chapter Seven, A Selection of Loans, for more information on this loan). Loans requiring only 3-5% down with good terms are widely available for owner occupants from almost any loan broker.

# Building Up Equity

Many people obtain their down payments for future rental properties by buying their own homes first with minimum down payments. They prepay their mortgages and build additional equity through appreciation. Then they have the choice of buying new personal residences and renting out their old houses, or they can refinance their homes and use the proceeds as down payments on rental properties.

This is how I obtained my first rental house. I purchased it to live in during the fall of 1992. I paid $97,000 and borrowed the down payment and closing costs from my mother. I lived in the house for a little over one year before I married and rented out my house. Voila! I had a rental property.

By the spring of 1998 my old home was worth $140,000 with a mortgage of $80,000, giving me $60,000 in equity. Yet I had put down no money of my own originally to buy this house. By borrowing against this equity I had enough money to buy a half share in another house with a friend. My personal home transformed itself into one and a half rental houses within five years. The increased rent on my old home (rental rates had risen along with property values) allowed me to easily pay both the old first mortgage payment and the new second mortgage payment.

You can see how this process of pulling money out of older rental properties can continue indefinitely. I have purchased other rental houses during the past five years, and each year another house has built up enough equity to allow me to get a new second mortgage. It's amazing to me how much easier it is to find more money to invest once the first few properties have had a chance to appreciate. The key is to acquire some properties in the first place.

## Saving Money

Saving is an old-fashioned method of acquiring enough capital to make investments. It works, but it can be slow in the beginning. As you buy properties each should produce cash flow for you to save, reducing the time you need to wait while you save up enough money for the next down payment. But getting to this delightful point in your investment career takes time, patience, and a clear focus on your long term goal. You must save up enough money to buy your first rental property before its cash flow can help you buy the next house.

Saving is a difficult thing to do. Why? Suppose you have $5,000 in your savings account. This money is earning perhaps 3% per year, or $150. You will also have to pay taxes on this interest income, leaving you with very little gain as a reward for your frugality.

In contrast think of all the lovely things you could buy with that $5,000. You and your spouse could go on a cruise in the Caribbean and still have enough left over for a ski vacation in the Rockies. Wouldn't you have fun telling your co-workers where you spent your vacations?

Or you could buy a new leather couch for the living room. It's so beautiful, and your parents are coming to visit, or your boss, or your best friend from high school - you fill in the blank. A leather couch would show them you've done well. And there would still be money left over to buy new drapes, a matching lounger, and a new coffee table.

Or you could fall prey to the lure of a new car. All families need a minivan, right? Only a few thousand dollars down, and you can own a depreciating asset that requires monthly payments. Not only can you spend your savings in one visit to the automobile dealer, you can prevent yourself from saving anything else for the next five years because you must make monthly car payments! Hard to resist a deal like that. Indeed, tens of thousands of new vans are sold each year on credit.

Saving today so you won't have to work tomorrow demands discipline. It requires the ability to see into the future. Saving can be fun if you believe that every dollar saved is helping you to buy your life back. Just like the Greek slave who could earn money and save it in order to buy his freedom, you can liberate yourself from the tyranny of earning a living. If you think of your savings this way, it may make being frugal almost as much fun as spending.

## It's Impossible to Save

Before you say it's impossible for you to save any money, I'd like you to look at your income. How much money have you earned over the last ten years? $200,000? $500,000? And how much will you earn in the next ten years? Wouldn't it be nice if you kept some of that money?

If you lack the discipline to pay yourself every month, you could try this trick. Go to your bank or credit union and get a vacation loan, perhaps for $5,000. Then don't go on vacation. Put the money into a savings account in a different bank. Then pay back your monthly vacation loan. When you've paid off the loan, you'll still have the $5,000. Next, repeat the process until you have enough to make a down payment on a house.

Will you pay a higher interest rate on the borrowed money than you're earning on the money in the savings account? Yes, but it's better to save the money somehow than not at all. Maybe once you get into the habit of writing a $350 monthly check to the bank on your loan, you won't need to get another vacation loan. You can continue writing the monthly check, but to yourself. Then deposit it into your special savings account.

My parents like to take cruises. One year they met a couple with an interesting story. This husband and wife agreed when they married that half of any raises he received would be spent, but the other half would be saved and invested in small apartment buildings. Though she stayed home with the kids, they still saved quite a bit of money. Eventually the cash flow from their apartment buildings was contributing substantially to their income.

They began to take three cruises a year. The husband's co-workers thought he must have gotten a big inheritance since they couldn't afford to travel as much as he did. But through the years his co-workers hadn't saved like he had. He had created his own financial windfall by making the decision to save and invest so many years ago.

## Unexpected Money

Mini-windfalls appear in people's lives quite frequently. Since people don't have a plan for unexpected monies, it is spent ineffectively, usually on consumer items. But for someone who has a goal, these windfalls can speed up a retirement plan drastically.

I know someone who purchased his personal residence just before a burst of appreciation gave him a substantial amount of equity within a short three years. He then borrowed against this equity to buy rental properties. A woman with whom I worked told me how she was unexpectedly fired from her part-time position as a bank teller when the bank was purchased in a bank merger. She was paid $25,000 in severance pay! Another woman I know received a chunk of money as an insurance settlement for being the innocent victim in a car accident.

All of these people received amounts well below $100,000. This money wasn't enough for them to retire, but it was sufficient to give a real boost to their financial status.

Some of my students assure me they would never be the recipients of a lump sum of money, but none of the events in the previous paragraph could have been predicted. They could happen to you. You want to be ready with a plan in case they do.

When I met my husband, I owned my own home plus a half interest in a house in Austin, Texas, with my twin sister. My route to owning a small real estate empire looked like a long one. But I was only 27. I had time on my side. And I really didn't have a lot of other choices. If I didn't save then and get started, when would I ever do it?

I figured I would be able to buy another house when I turned thirty. I would leap frog into a new home using owner occupied loan terms and would rent out my old house. It never occurred to me that within a short eight months after buying the house I planned to turn into my first rental I would meet the man of my dreams, accept his proposal, and be married.

It turned out Steven had money sitting in his savings account because of several recent bond redemptions he had been forced to accept. Instead of spending the money on fancy wedding rings or an elaborate honeymoon, we purchased two houses with low money down, non-qualifying loans in Texas with my sister and her husband as partners.

So not only did my real estate investment plans unexpectedly benefit when I fell in love, so did my sister's plans. She located two houses in the suburbs of Austin that needed cosmetic work plus a bit of serious fix up work. My husband Steven provided the money for the down payments and supplies, and Shelley and Brandon did the work. For them it was a no money down deal they couldn't have predicted. How could they have known that a future, unknown brother-in-law would want to invest with them? The unexpected can happen to you as well.

# Get a Partner

As the previous story illustrates, it's possible to find a partner who has the money to invest while you supply the know-how and handle the work. If you share your goals and talk about real estate throughout your day-to-day life, you will discover people who are interested in buying rental property with you. Depending on the current opportunities in your local market, you could buy fixer uppers like Shelley and Brandon did or you could buy premium condition houses in an appreciating market where you'll share the increase in equity with your partner. Your partner will supply the down payment while you handle the property management chores.

At some point you may find a house you want to own, but you don't have quite enough money to buy it by yourself. Once when my friend David was showing houses to a former student of mine, they invited me to come with them. The first house we walked into was perfect. It was only four years old, priced a bit under market, and was in great shape. The master bath had a separate tub and shower plus a walk-in closet, and several rooms in the house had vaulted ceilings. The deck in the backyard faced the mountains, and the house was in great condition. I knew all these features would make the property very desirable to tenants.

I turned to my former student as we stood in the living room about to leave, and asked him if he wanted to make an offer. He said no. He wanted to buy a house in a less expensive price range. So I turned to David and asked him if he wanted to buy the house with me. He was surprised. He knew I hadn't even been looking for a house. I didn't have enough money for a down payment. But I loved that house.

After making sure the client really didn't want to make an offer, David agreed that somebody should buy the house. We talked with our spouses and made an offer together for less than the already attractive asking price. Though the seller's agent told us that two full price offers had previously been rejected, the seller countered us at less than full price since we agreed to rent the house back to him for a few months until he could move into the new house he was having built.

A word of caution here: only take on partners whom you like and trust. Have a plan to dissolve the partnership if it turns out that the two of you do not work well together. If you can afford to buy a property by yourself, you will avoid the hassle of negotiating every decision with your partner. It will be solely up to you whether or not to build a deck, lower the rent, or lease to someone with pets.

Many real estate gurus warn against investing with partners because of potential disagreements. On the other hand a partner may care as much about the property as you do. She or he can be responsible for it when you go on vacation and vice versa. In appreciating markets buying with a partner allows you to avoid lost opportunity costs. Instead of losing the opportunity to make money while you wait to qualify for a loan by yourself, you can own a half interest in an appreciating house.

## Borrowing Money

Any asset you own can be used as collateral for a loan. You can borrow against your personal home. You can borrow against one of your rental properties. Banks will set up lines of credit using your stock certificates as collateral, and 401(k) plans will let you borrow against your retirement fund. Friends and family may even give you personal loans secured only by their faith and trust in you.

You should only borrow money if you are confident you can earn a higher rate of return on it than you will have to pay in interest. If you have to pay your mother 8% on the money she loans to you, your anticipated rate of return on that money when you invest it in real estate should be at least two to three times that amount, 16-24%.

Borrowing money does involve a degree of risk. You are leveraging your assets which will allow you to earn a higher rate of return, but you are also incurring a debt which will have to be repaid. It is important to know how you will obtain the necessary dollars to make the debt payments as they come due.

For the purposes of this book I am assuming you are borrowing money to buy rental property which will produce enough income to cover the payments on the borrowed money. If the income will not be enough to make the debt payments, you should probably find a different investment, or else wait until you've saved up additional money to put down.

Negative monthly cash flows are not fun and should be avoided. Sometimes you can fiddle with the numbers by paying interest only instead of paying both interest and principal on the borrowed money. This will make your payments smaller, but usually you will have to make a large balloon payment of the unpaid principal at some point in the future.

If you get a loan with a balloon payment, make sure that the balloon due date is in the distant future, at least five years away and preferably longer. Real estate values go in cycles. Just in case the market takes a dip at the same time your balloon payment is due, you'll want to build an escape clause into your loan allowing you to postpone the due date in exchange for paying a higher interest rate or a small flat fee.

You can refinance your personal residence in order to access some of your equity. As long as you resist the urge to finance out every cent, you'll still have equity in your home. Even though some lenders will lend up to the full value of your house, I suggest leaving at least 20% equity. This equity acts as an emergency cash reserve.

Some people have trouble with the idea of refinancing their homes or rental properties. After spending a couple of years watching the loan balances get smaller and smaller, they get bitten by the security bug. It can be quite reassuring to have a large equity position in your home and investment properties.

Unfortunately, your rate of return will get lower every year as your leverage decreases. It's much harder to reach your financial goal when you are earning 12% instead of 20% on your invested money. You need to acquire your target number of properties before you switch over to the "pay off all the loans stage". If you decide to focus on paying off one or two properties, the other properties you could have purchased will be escalating in value. By the time you are ready to buy your next house, it may cost far more than it does today.

Remember that each house you buy is a small money making machine. If your financial goal requires you to buy five houses, then the sooner you acquire them, the better. Your tenants will help you to pay them off, and you'll be enjoying any appreciation in your area instead of worrying about how you'll afford to buy your last house.

## Taking a Breather

Keeping yourself leveraged can become more difficult over time. As you get closer to acquiring your last house, you may discover that you've become more conservative since you began your investment career. Even though you were happy with high loan-to-value ratios at the beginning, you may be reluctant to return to those same high ratios after you've paid down some of your loans. It's different than it was in the beginning - you've got a lot more to lose now.

This situation happened to a couple I know. They wanted five and one half rental properties in addition to owning their personal residence. When they reached four and a half properties, they had the chance to buy another house at a below market price. But it would have required borrowing against one of their rental properties to get the down payment. That meant their cash flow from that property would have been drastically reduced because of the new mortgage payment. Even though the purchase of the new property would have brought their combined loan-to-value ratio for all their properties to only 70%, which would have left a 30% equity position (compared to the minimum of 20% I usually suggest), they decided to wait one more year to buy their last house.

Financially this was probably not the best decision to make. Houses in their target purchase area were appreciating rapidly, and they would be losing the chance to leverage their money more effectively. But sometimes you will need to take a breather on your road to retirement.

After spending one and a half years building a duplex from the foundation up and doing the vast majority of the work themselves, this couple was tired. They wanted to have a little fun to reward themselves for all their hard work. They wanted a chance to enjoy the cash flow they had built up, even if it meant delaying their retirement plans. They preferred to strengthen their financial situation by paying off two small construction loans before acquiring their final property.

Sometimes you will have to make a decision like this where you evaluate financial benefits against emotional desires. Particularly when it comes to borrowing money to continue an investment plan, one spouse may be resistant. It is better to come to an agreement that makes both spouses happy rather than to fight about it. Decisions cannot be made solely on a financial basis. Unity in the home is crucial to a successful investment career. If that means you'll have to wait an extra year or two before you retire, so be it.

# Moving

If you live where starter homes cost $300,000 and up, you may decide to move someplace where housing prices are more reasonable. Saving a down payment for a $100,000 house is much easier than for a $300,000 house.

To find a housing market you can afford may mean you have to move only a short distance. Even communities only twenty minutes apart may have housing prices which are dramatically different. Or you may decide to move to a different state.

For example, Boulder, Colorado, is located eleven miles away from the city of Broomfield, a suburb of Denver. In 1997 a 1,300 square foot house in Boulder cost $165,000 while a 1,300 square foot house in Broomfield cost $130,000.

The contrast in housing prices in different states can be even more dramatic. A 1,300 square foot house in a northern suburb of Austin, Texas, was even less expensive in 1997 with a price of only $90,000.

If you decide to look for a community which offers you a better chance to be a successful real estate investor, you should consider many different factors. Comparing housing prices is just the start.

Everyone is familiar with the typical qualities you should look for in a new community. Quality of life is dependent on good schools, convenient shopping, a strong job market, and recreation opportunities. These are items I feel you can judge for yourself, so I won't go into them in great detail. Just keep them in mind when you're considering where to move.

## Potential for Appreciation

You may want to look for an area which you believe will experience appreciation. An area which is experiencing an inward migration of people is more likely to appreciate than an area which is losing population, but even areas with exploding job and population growth may not experience the appreciation you may expect. An example of this phenomena is the Austin area. Prices were stagnant for houses located in the suburbs north of Austin in the mid-nineties.

When I began buying in this area in 1993 I thought Texas properties had more room to appreciate than did Colorado properties. Housing prices were less than their highs in the mid-eighties before the big plunge due to sharply dropping oil prices and the resulting damage to the Texas economy. In addition Austin had an unbelievable job growth rate, one of the top in the nation. Many high tech companies were building new facilities in Round Rock, a town on the northern edge of Austin.

What I didn't take into account was how many builders would leap at the chance to sell new homes to the new residents. Restrained by few growth limitations compared to the Denver metro area, houses sprang up like weeds. Prices on existing Austin homes remained stable while Denver prices kept going up. Fortunately, I owned houses in Denver as well as Austin.

On the other hand, if it's going to take you a few years to acquire your properties, moving to an area where the housing prices are flat could be beneficial. Instead of sadly watching prices rise while you save, it may be easier for you to live someplace where you can predict how much you'll need to buy another property in two years.

---

Many people confuse the rising cost of a median home in an area with appreciation. They read in newspaper articles that the median prices for homes in their city rose 6.7% in the last year. Hooray! they say. They think the value of their houses went up 6.7%. But the median price for houses sold in any given year may have no relation to the appreciation rate on existing houses.

A median price is the price at which half of all houses sold cost more and half of the houses sold cost less. The new houses being built in America are usually bigger than the older homes. At the very least they are constructed of brand new components which cost more than used components. So new houses cost more than the resale houses on the market. Whenever many new houses are being built, their higher sale prices will disproportionately increase the median sales price.

You need to look for the appreciation rate on existing home sales to find out what is happening to the values of your properties. The best way to do this is to request that your real estate agent run comps (sale prices for comparable homes) for the neighborhoods where you own properties.

If you are on the internet you can access the Bank of America web site, www.bankamerica.com, and run comps yourself if you live in one of the many states for which they have property sales information. These comps will show you if prices are going up for houses which are similar to your properties.

---

# Local Regulations

States and cities may regulate rental properties. Even if any resulting additional costs can be passed onto the tenants, these regulations usually result in more work and hassles for the landlady or landlord. An example is the city of Boulder, Colorado.

Rental properties in Boulder must regularly have a rental inspection in order to get a rental license. You must pay for the license. The housing inspector has the authority to require you to "improve" your property in order to get or renew your license. Whether you or your tenants think these improvements make the property safer is irrelevant. You will make any required changes and you will pay for them. Arguing about them may only result in the inspector going through all other properties you own in the city with a fine tooth comb. This happened to an investor I know. His advice is to grin and go along. Fighting a bureaucracy is a losing battle.

Other localities may have rent controls or are thinking about initiating them. To raise your rents may require the approval of some governmental body. If you don't like the idea of Big Brother supervising your investments, you should look for cities without housing departments.

Look in the phone book. Even if a housing department exists, you may still want to call them and discover exactly how big the department is. If it's small and has only a few rules which won't apply to you, you may decide to invest there. Just keep in mind that government has a way of growing.

## Taxes and Insurance

Some states have much higher property taxes than do others. In addition some states such as Texas charge investors higher taxes than homeowners. I learned about this the hard way. My sister and I assumed a mortgage on a house in 1993. The mortgage payment plus the taxes and insurance prorated monthly was low enough to give us a positive cash flow. But the next year when the taxing authorities discovered that the house had become a rental property, they changed our tax status and increased our tax rate.

To add insult to injury, the previous owner had been over sixty-five, so the annual tax amount the real estate agent had given us for the house was even lower than the normal homeowner rate because Texas discounts property taxes for older people. A double whammy! Our taxes shot way up. This property has been an alligator ever since, the only property I own where the rents and mortgages are upside-down. I have to pay money each month instead of receiving cash flow! Don't let something like this happen to you.

Insurance costs also vary from state to state. Insurance for a rental house worth $130,000 in the Denver metro area runs about $340 per year with excellent coverage. A house worth $90,000 in the Austin metro area will cost over $600 to insure, and the coverage, in my opinion, is not as good as what I'm getting in Colorado.

However, higher taxes and insurance will usually not affect your overall rate of return on your invested money. Rents in Austin are much higher in relation to the value of the properties than they are in Denver. Despite what lawmakers may think, it's the tenants, not the investors, who pay the additional costs to subsidize the low homeowner taxes.

So I'm not telling you to avoid high tax communities, but to be aware of the differences among states. Don't make a buying decision based on information that is true in your old state but not in the new state, or you may get to feed an alligator, too.

## Inheriting Money

The media reports that Americans are about to witness the biggest inter-generational transfer of assets in our history as a country. Some people, of course, will inherit a lot of money while others will inherit small amounts (or none at all), but just twenty-five thousand is enough for an investor down payment on a nice single family home in most parts of this country. Half of that amount is enough if you can find a trustworthy partner to buy a house with you on a fifty-fifty basis. A fraction of that will help you into an owner-occupied home.

The main problem with inheriting money is its uncertainty. When will you inherit? How much will it be? It's not prudent to make your retirement plans around an anticipated inheritance. My father has warned me in jest since I was a child that he planned to spend my inheritance. That was fine with me since I wasn't willing to wait for him to die before I became financially independent.

Yet some people do sit around like vultures, ignoring their responsibility to take care of their own financial fortunes. They forgo sacrifice and planning in anticipation of a large inheritance. Besides the ghoulish nature of waiting for an inheritance, you can't count on receiving it.

My great-aunt and uncle were some of the first people to build on Malibu Beach. How much was their small apartment building worth when they eventually passed away? A bundle, but as far as my family is aware, only the Catholic church benefitted.

The moral of this story? It's best to plan as if you will receive no inheritance. Then if you do, wonderful. Depending on how large it is you will be brought closer to financial independence. You might even achieve it instantly. But on the other hand, if your relatives live into their nineties and spend all their money, you will still be okay. It is possible to take care of your own financial future. An inheritance is just a lovely bonus.

## Life Insurance

Even if none of your relatives are rich, you may discover they had a life insurance policy and you are the beneficiary. While substantial insurance amounts usually come with an emotional loss, this money will at least help to secure your financial situation.

My recommendation here is not to make large investment decisions until you have had a chance to recover your emotional balance. Unless you are an experienced real estate investor who wants to forget your sorrow by diving into work, it may be best to wait at least a year before making any big decisions about investing your insurance money. You may not be getting great returns by letting your money sit in a money market account, but at least it is safe until you are emotionally ready to deal with it.

## Settlements

This is a litigation crazy country, yet some lawsuits are well founded. Unlike the huge settlements publicized by the media, most cases concern much smaller amounts of money. Minor accidents, sex or age discrimination at work, and product liability settlements may provide you with a small nest egg. When I was a real estate agent I met a number of people who had received modest settlements and used all or part of them to buy real estate.

# Lease Options

Lease options are a hot topic in the real estate investment community at this time. Seminar leaders talk about how lease options will make you rich without having to buy any property. By tying up a property in a lease option you risk only a small option fee and your time spent managing the property until the time comes when you exercise your option, take control of the property, and perhaps even sell it mere moments later to an eager buyer who pays you much more than you paid for the property.

This sounds wonderful, but I still don't like the idea of lease options. I think the gentlemen traveling the country giving lease option seminars are making their money from being speakers, not by doing lease option deals.

I have two problems with lease options. First, it's similar to when you ask sellers to carry back notes on their properties. In bad markets they are forced to consider this option. But with the current low interest rates combined with a strong economy, only sellers with awful properties will carry back a loan or accept a lease option.

And when I say awful properties, I'm not talking about diamonds in the rough. I mean properties with incurable faults, or faults that would cost an exorbitant amount of money to correct. Items such as dreadful locations or cracked foundations, or a structure so old no lender will give a loan on it.

Secondly, even if your area of the country has a real estate market so weak that sellers with decent properties will agree to lease options, you are setting yourself up for an unpleasant experience in the future. If the property's value doesn't go up and you don't buy it, the sellers won't be happy. Reasonable or not, they may decide to try to harangue you into buying the property or threaten to sue you. Unhappy people will do amazing things.

Or else the property's value will rise just as you had hoped. Now you want to exercise your option, but the seller can see the equity he or she will be losing. Some sellers will go along quietly and sell to you anyway. Others will decide it's worth it to take you to court and fight the option contract.

Will they win? Maybe. You may be portrayed as the sharp real estate investor who took advantage of an ignorant person. Or your contract may not stand up in court for some nitpicky reason. In any case the battle over the lease option will absorb your time and energy.

If you are determined to do lease options, do get competent legal counsel to review your contracts and your risks. Make sure extended lease options are legal and enforceable in your state. Lease options that allow you to exercise your option several years in the future may or may not be binding. Find out the legality of your contract before you spend years managing a property, possibly for free.

# Chapter Four
# Selecting Properties

Selecting the best properties to own is dependent on your personal goals and talents. People with home maintenance skills and plenty of time could consider fixer uppers. Busy executives may want to purchase townhomes or condominiums where the homeowners association handles all the exterior maintenance. Those investors looking for easy-to-manage properties where they can maximize their income will look for fairly new single family homes which will attract financially stable tenants.

Trade-offs appear when you compare the different types of properties. Each has its advantages and disadvantages. You should take a good look at yourself and try to match your preferences with the properties which will suit you best, but don't get bogged down trying to psychoanalyze yourself. In the worst case scenario you'll buy a property that you don't like and you will decide to sell it. That's okay. Buying property is not the same as getting married. You can change your mind and trade your equity into something different without too much trouble.

Sometimes people freeze when they set out to buy their first rental property. They want a super deal, but they don't have the experience to recognize whether they've found a bargain or a headache. This chapter will show you how to analyze a property so you can project how profitable it will be. I'll also give you basic guidelines to qualify properties plus share my personal preferences with you.

Many people want to know how to find deals comparable to the ones promised by the marketers of real estate programs advertised on television or through seminars. Yes, great deals do show up, but they are a lot rarer than these promoters say. After all, if great deals are so readily available, why are the promoters selling programs instead of buying more property?

In my experience the best way to make money in real estate on a part-time basis is to buy a property in great shape for close to market price. You should be able to realistically predict that this property will generate a 20% or better annual rate of return the first year you own it. After buying this first property you will use it as your benchmark when you shop for your next property. Try to get a better deal each time by using what you've learned. While I hope you do find one or more great deals during your investment career, it's okay to start out with a deal that's good enough.

## Single Family Homes

Single family homes are my favorite type of property. They are the best type of property for beginning investors. Why? Because they are plentiful, easy to purchase, and easy to sell. Lenders like single family homes, so it's relatively easy to get attractive loans to buy them. Most tenants prefer single family homes over other types of rental units. And if you get transferred or decide to liquidate your property investments, single family homes are readily marketable.

Single family homes also have disadvantages. If you own five different houses, each in a different area, it will take more time for you to handle routine maintenance chores than if you owned one small apartment complex. Apartments make it easier to hire an on-site manager, and may also produce a higher rate of return.

Despite these drawbacks I still recommend owning single family houses. A nice house with a reasonable rent will attract tenants who tend to be more desirable overall compared to tenants who rent smaller units. More affluent tenants tend to rent houses instead of apartments.

These tenants, in my experience, have a lower eviction rate. They have more financial options than do tenants in the lower financial brackets and they have more to lose if they let their credit records become marred. Therefore, they pay the rent more reliably.

## Different Types of Single Family Homes

Not all single family homes are equal. The least expensive homes are older properties. These homes have higher rent-to-property value ratios than newer, more expensive, properties. This makes it seem as if you'll receive a higher monthly cash flow on your invested money, but this perceived advantage can, and usually is, canceled out by additional maintenance costs. Besides having to spend more money on repairs, you will have to invest more of your time either doing the repair work yourself or hiring and supervising someone else to do it.

After a number of years spent fixing up older properties I've switched to investing entirely in newer single family homes. These properties do have smaller rent-to-property value ratios, but they tend not to have any expensive maintenance problems for many years. Also tenants love to rent newer houses. They like master baths which have bathtubs as well as showers. They like vaulted ceilings in the living room and lots of big windows. They also like double paned glass and modern insulation.

If it is possible in your area to buy newer houses in a lower price range, a price range where rent-to-property value ratios are the most profitable, great. Buy these houses.

If newer houses in your area are in a price range too high to make good rentals, you can look instead for over-improved older houses. Some owners will upgrade their homes far above the level of the neighboring houses, ignoring the fact that they have the only house in the subdivision with hardwood floors and fancy French doors off the dining room. It is unlikely that they will ever recuperate the full cost of installing these extras when they sell their property. The lower values of the houses surrounding their house will limit its top dollar price.

Over-improved properties can be great buys. You may pay a small premium compared to the sale prices of houses with the same floor plan, but you'll get a lot more for your money. You'll have an easier time finding tenants if you can offer features not usually found in that price range. Someday when you decide to sell this house, your property will out-compete surrounding houses.

## Brand New Houses

In the past I avoided buying brand new houses because of the hassle and expense of putting in the landscaping. If I've already put down 10% or 20% to buy the house, why would I want to invest another 5% or so to pay for a deck, lawn, bushes, and a tree? Instead, I've preferred to purchase nearly new houses which are two to four years old at the time I buy them. These houses have already been landscaped and require little additional work.

However, I put my first brand new house under contract in the spring of 1997. Two builders were doing different series of homes in a new subdivision. The least expensive homes could only be built in three areas of the subdivision. One area backed to a very large commercial building with noisy fans. Another area backed to a street. But the third area backed to some very large, awkwardly shaped housing lots.

The builder was asking the same prices for these houses regardless of the area. I knew that houses built in the third area which did not back to a noisy commercial building or onto a street would have a higher future resale value. Also, unlike a lot of Colorado houses, people living in the third area wouldn't be looking directly across their backyards straight into the windows of another house. The strangely shaped lots behind the third area would force any houses built there to be at an angle.

I told the students in one of my real estate investing classes about this intriguing situation, but no one offered the builder a contract for a house in the third area. Finally, I showed the land and the model home to a good friend. He and his wife agreed to buy a house with my husband and myself.

How did it all turn out? The developer decided that the strangely shaped lots were unworkable and instead created a strip of open space. Lots in this development which backed to open space usually came with a lot premium of $5,000, but the builder had already signed contracts for all the houses along this newly created open space. So the location became even better than I had anticipated.

Getting the landscaping installed was a hassle, no doubt about it, but worth it in the long run. I have a half share in a brand new house, one of the least expensive in the entire development, which also has one of the nicest locations. Besides backing to a small piece of open space, the house is only a block away from the community pool!

Overall, though, I still favor near new houses. It's much easier to buy a house that's ready to rent out without investing additional time. Unless you find a situation where you can get a new house that's worth more than what you're paying for it, I think it's better to let someone else buy the drapes and install the yard.

# Overly Expensive Houses

You also need to be careful not to buy houses which are too expensive. You've probably seen the pyramid that represents house buyers. There are far more buyers for starter homes at the broad base of the pyramid than for the multi-million dollar mansions located at the tiny tip.

This same pyramid exists for renters. There are many more renters at the bottom, less expensive, part of the pyramid. Because of the increased demand, these renters will pay a higher rent-to-property value ratio for an inexpensive rental. As you go up the pyramid the rent-to-value ratio will decrease until you will not be able to rent an expensive house for enough to give you a satisfactory rate of return on your investment.

Also, the people who rent the more expensive houses will probably not be good long-term tenants. They earn a lot of money and need a tax shelter. Most of them will buy their own homes as soon as their leases are up if not sooner. The cost of breaking a lease may be a lot less for them than the money they'll have to pay in taxes if they stay too long in a rental house.

If you are a real estate agent, you may not mind tenants who sign short-term leases if they agree to buy a house using you as their agent. Your commission may be enough compensation for the hassle of finding new tenants on a frequent basis.

If you're not an agent, then you may decide to charge higher rents for short-term leases. The problem with this idea is that most tenants will refuse to pay a large enough rent premium to make a short lease worthwhile. They don't understand that you don't enjoy the challenge of renting a house two or three times each year instead of only once. They won't care if you have to spend more money on ads and sacrifice another weekend touching up paint where their furniture banged it up as they moved their belongings in and out. Unless you are desperate to rent a property, perhaps because it's the middle of December and it's hard to find tenants, you should avoid short-term leases.

# Functional Obsolescence

Whatever properties you buy, keep in mind the concept of functional obsolescence. Thirty years ago it was okay in the Denver area for a house to have only a carport. Twenty-five years ago the new houses featured one car garages or even two car garages. Now two car garages are standard and three is considered luxurious.

The same situation has happened with bathrooms. My grandmother's house had a bath which was accessible only through the bedrooms with no direct access from a hallway. As time went by, houses were built with half baths located on the main floor. Then master bedrooms started to appear with private three quarter baths. Now many new houses are being built with five piece master baths. These bathrooms have a separate oval tub and shower plus two sinks and a walk-in closet.

In either of these examples the older houses are less desirable not only because of their age, but because they lack features expected in a modern property. This same problem occurs in apartment units without room to install microwave ovens or enough counter space for the numerous modern appliances Americans own today. These problems are built-in and can be costly or impossible to fix.

Always try to buy properties which are as close to the current standards as possible. In any given price range some houses have more desirable features than do others. It's hard to predict future trends, but I think people will continue to want multi-car garages, nice master baths, and kitchens with plenty of space. Personally I've noticed a sharp upswing in the demand for air conditioning over the past few years.

At the 1998 International Builder's Show the following trends were noted. Home buyers, and presumably tenants as well, are looking for kitchens with islands, space for multiple cooks, large pantries, some sort of visual connection with the family or great room, plus a window above the sink.

Also popular are main level master bedrooms, media rooms for a home theater system, and higher ceilings for a feeling of spaciousness. In terms of neighborhood amenities parks and walkways are replacing preferences for tennis courts or swimming pools. The more features that modern buyers/tenants want that are present in or around your properties, the longer it will take before the properties become functionally obsolescent and less desirable to tenants.

# Getting a Discount

After a few years spent buying dumps, fixing them up and selling them, I switched to buying houses in great shape that I could rent immediately. However, I still like getting some sort of discount when I buy. I've discovered three common and easy ways to get a discount from some special sellers.

### Flexible Seller #1

The first type of flexible seller are the homeowners who are building a new house. John and Patti Smith have a long time, maybe four to six months, to sell their current home before the new one will be ready. It seems as if they are in a good position to hold tight and get their full price.

In actuality these sellers have a big worry - what will they do if someone buys their old house before the new one is ready? No builder is dumb enough to set a final closing date until the new house is almost ready for delivery, yet how many buyers of the seller's old house will be willing to buy it without knowing when they will get possession?

Most people looking for a home will want to move in as soon as they close, forcing John and Patti to make a double move complete with two kids, one cat, and a household of valuable furniture. This double move will cause havoc in their lives and cost them money. If instead they wait for the builder to give them a final closing date, they may not have enough time to get their old house sold and then they'll lose the new house. These sellers are between a rock and a hard place.

You, the friendly investor, can be the perfect solution to their problem. You will close on the sale of the old house well before the estimated completion date for the sellers' new home. Until the new house is ready, the sellers will rent back their old home from you.

This is where something strange happens. John and Patti will not want to pay you market rent for the property. Market rent is almost always far higher than the mortgage payment they are used to paying. They will balk at the idea of paying you $300 extra for two months, but instead they will agree to knock thousands of dollars off the price of their house.

Financially this reasoning makes no sense, but I've seen it over and over again. Sellers understand monthly payments because they are used to paying their mortgages on the first, but the equity tied up in their home seems like funny money. They don't hold onto it as tightly.

It's easy to find out if sellers are having a new house built. The multiple listing ad may mention a delayed closing date or ask for a rent-back agreement. If you meet the sellers when you are looking at the house, they will be happy to tell you why they are moving because they are so excited about their new home.

If nothing is mentioned in the advertising material and you never get a chance to talk to the sellers, have your agent mention to the listing agent that you are thinking about making an offer. In order to make it as attractive to the sellers as possible, you want to know what closing date the sellers would prefer since you've got some flexibility. Listing agents will generally volunteer the uncertainty about the closing date in response to this question.

## Making the Offer

When you make your offer write in the provision that the contract is contingent upon buyer and seller signing a lease back agreement within a short period of time after signing the sales contract. Don't include your entire lease as part of the negotiation at this point because a long lease in addition to the contract may confuse the sellers.

Focus instead on the modest rent the sellers will owe each month for the first two or three months of the lease, and then include something that says the rent will go to market rent of X dollars after that point in time. After all, you don't want a permanent tenant at below market rates in case the new house deal falls through and the sellers are forced to stay in their old home for a while. Also, when you point out what the market rate is, the sellers will be able to appreciate what a great rent you are offering.

You should also specify that the sellers must give you a certain amount of notice before they move, preferably at least thirty days since that's probably the notice the builder of their new home will give them. Put into your contract and later into the lease that the sellers will allow you to show the house to prospective tenants after they have given you the thirty day notice. Make sure the sellers are motivated to honor their agreement by including in your lease the right to hold a security deposit.

## Flexible Seller #2

A new home builder's nightmare is to have a buyer's loan denied right before closing. The builder has a finished home with high monthly carrying costs sitting in inventory. If that builder knew someone who could close FAST, there is room to negotiate on the price, even in a hot real estate market.

Denver has enjoyed a robust real estate market during the nineties, but I've been offered attractive terms when I've let on-site salespeople for builders know that I'm an investor who can get a loan quickly. Do they have any deals that are about to crash and burn? Would they like to keep my card in case of future emergencies? A few questions when you're out looking at new homes may save you thousands of dollars.

## Flexible Seller #3

The people who own houses next door to your rentals may tell you they want to sell before they talk to an agent, offering to share with you the amount they save by not having to pay a commission. But usually you can do even better than that by making them a low offer. You tell them you know it's low, and you wish them the best of luck in getting more. But if they should decide they need to sell fast, they should give you a call. And in the meantime, they should write into any listing contract with an agent a provision that states that if they sell the house to you, they won't owe the agent a commission.

This has worked very well for me. On one occasion some neighbors wanted $139,900 for their house. I thought the house was worth $138,000. I told the sellers I would be willing to pay them $132,000, but wished them luck in finding someone who would pay more. A month later both of the sellers had lined up jobs in their home state of Minnesota, and they needed to sell fast. They called me, I showed my husband the house, and we bought it for $132,000.

This type of situation comes up with people other than the neighbors of your rentals. Anybody who knows you are an investor may ask you to consider buying their house. So let the world know you are in the market for rental houses. You can save thousands of dollars by broadcasting this tidbit of information far and wide.

# Condominiums and Townhouses

Condominium and townhouses are called attached housing. It's generally easier to get financing for these units if they are built townhouse style. Townhouse style means your unit may share side walls, but no unit is above or below your unit. Homeowners associations usually handle most or all of the exterior maintenance, but sometimes the property owner is responsible for the roof maintenance and exterior painting. Always check the covenants before you buy so you aren't surprised by unexpected responsibilities and expenses.

Buying attached units may be your best choice if you have little spare time. Neither you nor your tenants will have to worry about shoveling walks, mowing grass, or doing exterior maintenance, but you will have to pay the monthly homeowners association fee. If you lose or quit your job, you will not have the option of handling your own maintenance in exchange for not paying your monthly fee. You will also have little control over how the association fees are managed and spent unless you are willing to join the board in charge of making the group spending decisions.

The biggest drawback to buying attached housing is its price volatility. In a weak real estate market the prices of attached units fall faster and further than do the prices of single family homes. On the other hand, these prices will also appreciate faster when the market strengthens again.

What does this mean for you? You should probably not buy attached housing in an up market. Your downside risk is much greater than it would be if you owned single family homes. If your area is experiencing a down cycle, wait until prices seem to have bottomed out, then load up on as many attached units as you can prudently afford. When the market recovers, you'll get a higher rate of appreciation on your money invested in attached housing than you would on single family houses.

In the late eighties oil prices dropped sharply. People who worked in oil dependent states such as Texas, Oklahoma and Colorado lost their jobs. Some moved away to take new jobs. Others couldn't afford to make their house payments. Foreclosure rates skyrocketed as housing units were dumped on the market. Real estate prices weakened, then sank.

I was in college at this time. With a limited income and no savings I couldn't take advantage of the situation. I knew a successful businessman, however, who decided to visit a brand new condominium complex near his office. Units which had been selling for $65,000 were available for only $45,000. He eagerly bought four units.

But prices continued to drop. Soon units with two bedrooms were selling for $22,000 and one bedroom units were selling for $17,000. Due to the monthly homeowners association fee, it was hard to rent the properties for a positive cash flow even at prices this low. Why? Because potential renters were either buying properties at bargain prices, or they were negotiating hard with property owners.

Instead of panicking because his first four units had dropped in value by more than 50%, Jerry bought another thirteen units in this same complex. Unwilling to manage the units himself, he hired a property manager. The management fees on top of the other costs produced a negative cash flow every month. Fortunately, he could afford the small monthly alligator produced by the combination of high expenses and low rents.

After a few years the market turned around. Prices and rents both went up. Soon the properties were producing a cash flow of over $50,000 per year. When Jerry retired, this extra income allowed him to enjoy a comfortable lifestyle. He's been leasing a brand new Cadillac every two years and taking three cruises annually. In the fall of 1997 he and his wife treated all five of their children and their children's spouses, plus the grandchildren, to a cruise in the Caribbean. Jerry's patience and the courage he displayed by investing in condominiums in a down market paid off handsomely.

If your area is experiencing an up real estate market, but you don't have the time to take care of single family homes, attached housing may still be your best option. Look for units which are as nice as houses. Units with garages are best. Luxurious master baths will always be in demand. Basements offer valuable storage. People also prefer end units because they have neighbors on only one side.

You should probably avoid converted apartments in most cities. These are usually the least desirable of all attached housing. Their prices are the first to suffer in a down market and are the last to recover. In addition many lenders will refuse to provide financing for converted units. In general, you should buy converted apartments only if they are highly desirable in your area.

## Duplexes, Triplexes and Four-plexes

The biggest advantage of these small multi-unit properties is their financing. Unlike large complexes which require commercial financing, you can buy these properties using owner occupant or investor residential financing.

The biggest drawback is trying to find small multi-unit properties in good locations. Zoning tends to cluster these types of properties in unappealing settings. I've seen many side streets filled with tacky looking four-plexes. The front yards are nonexistent, sacrificed to make room for parking spaces. The tenants' cars look like they've seen much better days and everything feels dirty. Who would want to live in an area like this? Not you nor anyone else who is likely to keep a rental unit in good condition.

You may find an exception to the situation I've just described, a nice small multi-unit located in a pleasant residential neighborhood. That property would most likely be a good one to own. Do, however, avoid other properties which are surrounded by an entire trashy block. You could fix up your building to look nice, but it won't help if all your neighbors don't care about their properties.

Many people I talk with are convinced they can make a ton of money by owning a duplex or four-plex. They assume multi-units are always profitable so they don't bother to look at the rate of return numbers. They often end up paying far more for a property than its rents will justify. I'm not sure where this idea that multi-plexes are always incredibly profitable comes from, but it isn't necessarily true.

If you want to buy a multi-plex, do the numbers. You're investing to make money. Since your units will be inexpensive compared to single family housing, you may not get tenants who are as financially stable. Even if they have finances like the Rock of Gibraltar, you will still probably have to spend more time managing the property. After all, if a four-plex costs $300,000, and two single family homes would cost $150,000 apiece, then you're going to have twice as many tenants for the same total investment. Your rate of return must be higher than you could get buying single family homes to make it worth your while.

## Apartment House

Buying apartment houses is not the focus of this book though much of the information provided will still apply. Owning an apartment house generally requires a higher level of management skill. Rates of return can be quite attractive, but managing many small units is a full-time job. Eventually, if your property is large enough, you'll be able to afford to hire a resident manager, but that may be years away.

Just as with small multi-unit buildings, the supply of small apartment houses is limited. You will have to look in a larger market area, perhaps buying a building that is not located close to your own home.

The best opportunities for profit occur if you are willing to take on a problem building. One of my students told me about a building with approximately thirty units he bought on the opposite side of Denver from where he lived. One tenant was using a ground floor unit as a drive-up drugstore for illegal drugs. Other tenants were equally shady.

The seller wanted out and was flexible on the financing terms and purchase price. Though my student would have preferred a building that was closer to his home, he wanted a property he felt he could improve for profit.

For the next two years he drove to the apartment house almost every day to handle evictions, repairs, and to show the property to new tenants. Over time he eliminated the bad tenants and replaced them with good tenants. Though this man does not intend to keep the building forever because of the large amount of time it requires, he should do very well when he decides to sell. His building is a far more attractive and valuable investment property now than when he bought it.

## Falling in Love

Most real estate investment books will tell you to look only at the numbers on a property. Whether you personally like the property is supposed to be beside the point.

But as a small investor looking to purchase five or so properties, you can and should really like your rental units. Feel free to buy houses with views of the mountains or the lake. Admire the five piece master bath. Marvel at the feeling of spaciousness created by the vaulted ceiling. You'll be proud of your properties and tenants will be eager to live in them.

All houses are NOT created equal. Some have very small backyards while others have yards which are difficult to reach because there is no back door. Some lots back up to a four lane street or a highway. These types of backyards aren't positive features. Home buyers want private backyards with easy access and so do tenants.

I've seen the dumbest things. Narrow, twisting staircases in houses less than five years old, floor plans that made no sense, houses with windows only on the north side, and houses located next to busy streets or commercial buildings. On paper these houses look fine because the agent writing the description neglects to mention the problems. When your agent shows you the properties, you discover that they aren't nearly as nice as you anticipated.

It's okay to look at fifty houses to find the one that sings, though it usually takes me no more than twenty before I find one I want to buy. I listen for the music when I step into a house. Maybe the house is smaller than what I would want to live in, but that's okay. Would it be ideal for some potential tenants? Would this darling two bedroom, two bath house be perfect for a single person, two roommates, or a single parent? Is this four bedroom house located in a popular school district so families with children would want to live in it? And most of all, would tenants who take pride in their homes want to live there?

# Fixer Uppers

I'm a fixer upper at heart. I adore the idea of taking a dump and turning it into a beautiful home. Unfortunately, very few dumps are worth the time and effort it will take to get them into tip-top shape.

Why are fixer uppers usually not worth buying? There are two reasons. First, as we discussed earlier, you make more money if you own rentals which are near the bottom of the price pyramid, but these properties are the worst ones to buy to fix up.

Why? Because lots of people enjoy fixing houses. They dream about making money through sweat equity. So fix up properties are in demand, especially at the low end of the market. A property which will sell fixed up for $130,000 will sell quickly at $120,000 in shabby condition in a good real estate market.

But after you spend $2,000 for the new carpet, $1,000 for the new vinyl, $500 for new paint, $1,000 to redo the bathroom, $1,500 for a new furnace to replace the old one which has a cracked heat exchanger, plus $1,000 to fix the deck and $300 for new landscaping, the profit you can earn will be small compared to the amount of time you've invested. And if you live in the property while you fix it up, you'll have the stress of living in an on-going project. It's hard to relax when you're surrounded by endless things to do.

The best properties to buy for fix up are those properties located further up the price pyramid. If starter homes are selling for $130,000, then you should be looking at houses which will sell for $250,000 after you've fixed them up. The people who usually buy houses in this middle price range are not interested in earning sweat equity. They already have high paying jobs. What they want are houses that look great from the moment they buy them. These buyers are willing and capable of buying houses in top condition.

Now you bump into the second problem with fixer uppers. If you fix up a property in this higher price range, it won't be in the ideal price range to keep as a rental. Your best option may be to rent it out for a year to establish it as an investment property, then 1031 tax exchange your equity into one or two smaller houses which would be more profitable long-term rental properties. You could also sell the property immediately, but then you may incur a higher tax liability since you haven't held the property for very long.

After fixing up a couple of low end properties, I've switched to buying houses which are as close to perfect as I can find. I don't want to invest either my time or additional equity into these houses. I want to set up my retirement with as little effort as possible. Since all houses need regular maintenance, why start out with problems? There are always more problems and more expenses than expected.

Even so, I would like to do some more fix up projects in the future. I'm waiting for the real estate market to cool down. In a slow market only the houses in the nicest condition sell. Dumpy properties sit on the market, and if the seller really needs to sell, the price comes down. This is when buying dumps at the low end of the market can be profitable. Until then I'll stick with ready-to-rent houses.

## The One Percent Rule

I've told you to buy properties that you love, but you also need to buy properties that make financial sense. You need a way to compare one property to another. Should you buy the two bed-room house in the prestigious area or the three bedroom house in the little town twenty minutes away?

Some authors will give you rules to follow. The 1% rule is particularly popular. Supposedly if you buy a property for $100,000, you should be able to rent it for at least $1,000 per month. If you can't, then you shouldn't buy that property.

There is a major problem with this rule; it only works in states with high property taxes and insurance. It does not work in states with low property taxes and insurance. The authors who promote this rule have invested in states where this rule works, and they assume it works everywhere else in the United States as well. Not true! You'll have to do the numbers for your area to see if this rule makes sense where you live

Let's take a look at two properties I own. One is located in Texas and the other in Colorado. Each house was built in the early eighties. They both have approximately 1,300 square feet with three bedrooms, two bathrooms, and a two car garage. Given the price differences between Texas and Colorado, the Texas house is worth $90,000 while the Colorado house is worth $130,000, but both are starter homes for their respective areas.

The Texas house rents for $895 per month which is darn close to meeting the 1% rule, but the Colorado house only rents for $1,100. According to the 1% rule, I should be buying all my houses in Texas instead of Colorado. But wait. How much are my property taxes and insurance for each of these houses?

|  | Texas | Colorado |
|---|---|---|
| Property tax | $1,998 | $927 |
| Insurance | $609 | $332 |
| Total | $2,607 | $1,259 |

The property taxes and insurance are more than twice as much for the less expensive Texas house. Much of the extra rent I don't receive on the Colorado property is compensated for by the money I save on taxes and insurance. So the 1% rule is area specific. It may not work where you live. Then how should you evaluate properties?

# Rates of Return

If you project your rates of return for two properties, it will be easy to compare them. You want to know what your annual rate of return will be on your invested money if you bought each property. If you think you can earn 25% the first year on property A or 28% on property B, all other things being equal you should buy property B.

How do you project your anticipated rate of return? Use the worksheets provided in the Appendices. The maintenance cost worksheet in Appendix B will help you to predict the expenses you would have for each property averaged over ten years. This figure is your anticipated average annual maintenance expense.

Next complete the rate of return worksheet in Appendix D. Call the tax assessor for tax rates and the percentage of the purchase price attributed to the improvements so you can calculate your depreciation amount. Call your insurance agent for a rough quote on each property and do some research to come up with the rents you think you can charge. Ask your lender or real estate agent to help you with the loan payments for principal, interest and any mortgage insurance premiums. The lender can also tell you the down payment and closing costs you will need to get a loan. The real estate agent should be able to help you project what appreciation, if any, you can expect in the near future.

When you've completed the rate of return worksheet for both properties you'll be able to compare the projected rates of return you would receive. True, your projections are based on a lot of educated guesses about maintenance costs, future appreciation, the stability of interest rates if you are getting an adjustable rate loan, plus how much rent you'll receive. But if you are consistent in your approach, you should be able to at least compare these two properties against each other to determine which one would be the better purchase.

If the difference in the projected rates of return is dramatic, you might want to recheck your numbers and the assumptions you made. Did you make a mistake either for or against one of the properties? If your numbers stand up to review, you should buy the property with the higher projected rate of return if the properties are comparable. Of course, you may be willing to accept a lower rate of return for a property located conveniently close to your home or work, or if it is in some other way particularly desirable to you.

## Rent-to-Property Value Ratios

A standard rent-to-property value ratio such as the 1% rule is not a valid guide to buying property throughout the United

States, but ratios between rents and property values can still be useful. These ratios are most revealing when you compare the rent-to-property value ratios of communities which have the same property taxes and insurance rates.

Let's look at two cities in Colorado. Boulder and Westminster are located only twenty minutes apart. They are in different counties, but Boulder County and Jefferson County have approximately the same property tax rates. Insurance rates are also comparable for properties with the same value.

But the rent-to-property value ratios in these two cities are quite different. If you bought a house in 1997 for $160,000 in Boulder, it would rent for $1,150 per month. Dividing $1,150 by $160,000 produces a .72% rent-to-property value ratio. A house which cost $160,000 in Westminster would rent for $1,300 a month. Dividing $1,300 by $160,000 produces an .81% rent to value ratio. If you wanted cash flow, you would get more per invested dollar by buying the property in Westminster.

So why do some people choose to invest in Boulder? Because they think properties in Boulder will appreciate faster than properties in Westminster. Perhaps this will happen, but it won't matter if they can't afford to keep their properties while they wait for this appreciation to occur. Cash flow can be the difference between staying in the business long enough to get rich, or being forced to sell if you find yourself in a financial bind.

So if you are deciding between two properties located in different areas, I think you should favor the property which produces more cash flow. While the total rate of return is important, including projected appreciation opportunities, cash in hand every month is the best type of return. Money in the pocket can solve many short-term problems, and it makes owning real estate a lot more fun.

# Deciding Between Two Available Properties - The Shortcut Method

If you don't want to take the time to analyze the projected rate of return numbers for two properties, you can use a more intuitive method instead to decide which one to buy. Let's say you are looking at two houses. One house has two bedrooms and a loft, a two car garage, and one and a half bathrooms. You like the layout, though the yard really needs a deck to make it attractive to either tenants or future buyers. The asking price is $135,000.

The other house has three bedrooms, a full bath, a three quarter master bath, and a three quarter bath in the basement. The layout is attractive, the yard has a deck, and the garage is a double. This house is the same age as the first one, seven years old. The price is $148,000. Which of these two houses would be the best one for you to buy?

First, ask your real estate agent or lender to tell you what the difference in the monthly payments would be. Let's say that including principal, interest, taxes and insurance, the second house will cost you $100 more per month.

Now ask yourself: If you were a renter who had $100 flexibility in how much rent you could afford to pay, how much more would you be willing to pay for the second house compared to the first? If the difference is more than $100, you should buy the second house. If it's less than $100, you should buy the first house.

# Magic Price Point

When you shop for houses in the lower price ranges you'll notice that a ten or fifteen thousand dollar difference in price will equal a huge difference in the type of house you can buy. This is why home buyers (and renters) in the lower price ranges stretch themselves to their financial limits when they look for a home.

The example I just used of a two bedroom house asking $135,000 and a three bedroom house asking $148,000 is based on two houses I showed to a buyer on February 1, 1998. The thirteen thousand dollars difference in price equaled a third bedroom, a master bathroom instead of a shared one, plus an extra bathroom in the basement for guests.

When the buyer and I looked at houses which cost an additional thirteen thousand, that is $161,000 instead of $148,000, we didn't find such a contrast in features. The individual rooms became bigger or the architecture had expensive details, but the actual number of bedrooms and bathrooms and garage spaces stayed the same. Since a larger room size or stained trim is not as important as a private master bath or a third bedroom, this price increase didn't add key features.

The magic price point where a house became noticeably more desirable was somewhere between $135,000 and $148,000 for the city of Littleton. You should be able to find this same type of price point in your neighborhood, adjusting for the different prices in your area. If you can afford to buy just above this price point, that's the best single family home to buy.

Why? Because neither renters nor future buyers will have to compromise on basic desirable features when they look at your house. Someone who can only afford to rent a house without a master bathroom will want to move up to renting a house which has that private bath as soon as they can. A renter who already has all the minimum features expected in a modern American house, however, will not bother with moving until he or she is ready to buy.

If a potential tenant or buyer can afford to go to the other side of the magic price point, they will. This means that the second house in my example will always be easier to rent or to sell, saving you time and money. And the tenants you get will be more likely to stay for a couple of years. Therefore if you can afford it, buy a house above the magic price point.

# Properties with Two Bathrooms

I look for properties with two bathrooms, meaning at least two toilets and preferably two showers. The cutest little house in the world won't interest me for long if there is only one bathroom. Why? Because if the only bathroom in a property develops a problem, the tenants are correct if they think that this is an emergency. Since tenants notice problems when they are home, which is usually during the weekends and in the evenings when plumbers charge special rates, a one bathroom house emergency can get expensive to fix. If your property has a second bathroom which is functional, then the plumber can be scheduled for regular business hours.

If you are buying smaller units, such as one bedroom condominiums or apartment buildings with many small apartments, you will have units with only one bathroom. This is unavoidable. Up your budget for plumbing repairs accordingly.

# Moving to a Different City or State

It's possible in many areas of this country to buy property which will produce cash flow with 20% down or break even with only 10% down, but you may live somewhere with extremely high prices and low rent-to-property value ratios. Even with the current low interest rates, starter homes in your area would produce no monthly cash flow or a negative cash flow even if you put down 20%. In addition, you're scared to buy in a housing market where the prices seem unbelievably high. You don't want to buy right before the local real estate market crashes.

If you are serious about investing in real estate, you may decide to move somewhere else. Maybe it would be worth it to take a job for less pay if you could move somewhere with a lower cost of living. Have you been dreaming about moving someplace far away from the rat race once you've made it financially? Maybe you should advance the time table for your moving plans.

If you've been offered a transfer, don't just tour around with an agent looking at homes you could buy. Also look at homes for rent and do some projected rate of return calculations. Ask your agent about state and local laws regarding rental properties. Is this state a property owner friendly state? Once you add in the benefits of moving someplace where rentals are profitable, an only okay job offer could become really tempting.

If you're not willing to move, perhaps you should broaden the area where you are looking for potential rental properties. Sometimes you don't have to go very far. The city limits of Boulder and Westminster are only twelve miles apart, yet the rent-to-property value ratios are quite different. Even if you chose to live in an expensive area, you could own properties in a nearby, less expensive, community.

## Buying in a Different State

Sometimes people fall prey to the grass is greener somewhere else syndrome. They aren't willing to move to this other place, but they want to invest there. They project rates of return that are so attractive it won't matter that they have to pay someone else to manage their properties for them.

Perhaps this other place really is a much better place to invest than where you live, but I have strong reservations about this idea. It's too easy to be overly optimistic about an area you don't know. Since you don't live there, you haven't learned about the problems. Instead you'll have to rely on someone else, probably someone who will make money if you decide to buy, to help you evaluate the investment possibilities. Unless you are investing with a local partner whom you trust explicitly as I have done with my twin sister in Texas, greed for high rates of return may lead you into bad situations that are made far worse by distance.

# Looking with an Agent

Finding a good agent can be difficult. When my sister moved to Texas she told many agents that she planned to buy a number of rental properties. Since in the beginning she hadn't actually bought any, we understood when none of the agents seemed excited. But when she told them she had purchased three houses in the past six months, and she wanted to buy three or four more, we were surprised when the agents failed to follow up.

Why did this happen? Because most agents are looking for the best buyer they can find, preferably someone who needs to buy within two months because their lease ends or their old house is being sold or the company paid housing allowance is about to expire. In contrast, an investor doesn't have to buy. Agents also worry that investors are looking for the impossible to find fabulous deals. If all the investor does is look without buying, the real estate agent will have wasted time and energy showing property. Unless the market is slow, many agents prefer to work with home buyers, not investors.

What can you do? You can ask people you know to refer you to agents. Agents like getting referrals so they take more care with referred clients. They know that if they don't, the flow of referrals might stop. So even if they aren't sure how serious you are, they may still be willing to invest some time in you in order to keep the referring person happy.

You can also find agents by calling on ads in the paper or by going to open houses. Look for a good click between you and the agent. Do you trust this person? Do they seem to know what they are talking about? Does the agent own rental properties? An agent who is a property owner can tell you what the market rents are based on experience and can better help you project your rates of return.

Some investors don't want to work with agents who are also investors. They are convinced that the agents will keep all the good deals for themselves. This is partially true. The agents will buy any super deals if they can afford to do so. If you want a super deal, you'll have to find it yourself. But if you want a good value, a house in good condition at just below market price, agents can be a great source of leads and a lot of help in getting the deal closed.

## Helping Your Agent

You can make your agent's job easier if you are willing to take a list of houses she or he gives you and drive by the houses without the agent in tow. As long as your local market isn't hot, you can receive a faxed list of new properties two or three times a week and have time to do a drive-by before scheduling a showing with the agent.

You can also tour the open houses each weekend. This will help you discover the neighborhoods you like. Agents don't want to hear that you are willing to look at anything. They want a specific target. If you can tell them where you would like to buy, that's a great help.

Remember, do not get so excited at an open house that you write an offer with the agent who is sitting there. If another agent has been working with you, and you think she or he is competent, call that agent to write up the offer. If your agent isn't available, and you're worried that someone else might make a competing offer that same day, ask another agent in your agent's office to help you. Explain to them that you are working with someone else, but need their help today. The agents can work out how to share the commission later.

## Buyer's Agent

Hiring a buyer's agent is generally a good idea. If an agent knows that you will buy through him or her, then it makes sense to invest time in you. In the beginning you may want to sign a short-term contract to use this agent, perhaps for one month. If you like the agent you can always extend the agreement.

# What If Your Agent Doesn't Do a Good Job?

Sometimes agents will insist on long-term buyer agency agreements. What happens if you sign a buyer agency contract and later decide that the agent isn't giving you enough attention? Or that the agent isn't competent?

In most states it is very easy for the consumer to break a buyer's agency agreement. If you feel you aren't getting good service, write a letter to the real estate company's broker and tell him or her that you want to break the agreement based on the agent's failure to do his or her part as an agent. Specify exactly what you want that you aren't receiving.

The managing broker may tell your agent to get with it or may ask you to work with a different agent. If the agent you signed up with is also the broker, then you can write a letter to him or her directly. If service doesn't improve, insist on the agent agreeing to terminate the contract. If the agent refuses, call your state's real estate commission. The people there can tell you exactly what your rights are and how to assert them.

Only in the worst case situation would you have to consult a lawyer. Most agents are very concerned about making their customers happy and will respond quickly to clearly presented complaints. Assuming that your agent is not a good agent, merely mentioning that you will be calling the real estate commissioner may be enough to get them to cooperate in releasing you from your contract.

# Chapter Five

# Loans

Most people have gone through the loan application process at least once, yet they don't understand exactly how the lender qualified them. They know it has something to do with their income and their debts, but how this information is transformed into a maximum loan amount is unclear.

This chapter shows how lenders qualify borrowers and how you can find lenders with more generous qualifying standards. We'll also discuss the different kinds of loans which are available. Discussing loans means talking about numbers, but don't worry. If you don't like math, that's okay. You can let the lenders tell you how much you can borrow without doing the numbers yourself, but you should understand this important fact: different types of lenders qualify borrowers using different criteria. So if one lender won't give you a loan, others may be willing to let you borrow from them.

Before you start going from one lender to the next, you need to know how to tell if two lenders are the same type of lender or different. Otherwise you'll waste your time. You may think that by asking five lenders for a loan and being turned down by all of them that you've explored five lending opportunities. But if these five lenders all use the same qualifying requirements, you may as well have talked to only one.

You should talk to a few lenders. Even if the first lender you talk with tells you they will give you a loan, their loan may not be the best one for you. Another lender may be offering a different loan you would prefer if only you knew it existed. You can't rely solely on your real estate agent to direct you to the best or most flexible lenders in town. Many agents are not familiar with the more unusual loans which are available.

Loans can be divided into three broad categories: government backed FHA and VA loans, conforming and non-conforming conventional loans which are frequently referred to as Fannie Mae loans, and portfolio loans. Different lenders or mortgage brokers will offer loans in one or more of these categories. For clarity's sake, I will discuss the lenders/mortgage brokers as if each offers loans in only one category.

FHA (Federal Housing Authority) and VA (Veterans Administration) loans offer very low to zero down payments. Mortgage insurance premiums or funding fees are charged to the borrowers to insure these loans since the down payments are so small. These loans are generally offered only to owner occupants though FHA does offer some special loans designed for investors which require larger down payments than for owner occupant loans.

One popular FHA program, the 203(k) loan program designed for fixer uppers, has been put on hold for investors because of problems with people misusing it. Check with your local Housing and Urban Development office for information on the current situation.

Most real estate agents can help you with questions you have about FHA or VA loans. The qualifying ratios for these loans are handled similarly to the conventional loans (ratios are discussed in more depth later in this chapter). Because the government programs come with large funding fees or upfront mortgage insurance costs, you should try to get a conventional loan instead whenever possible.

Conventional lenders require minimum down payments of 3-5% for owner occupants and 10-20% for investors. Some conventional lenders strictly follow Fannie Mae guidelines when they originate conventional loans. These loans are frequently called conforming conventional loans. If you as a borrower can meet the guidelines, you will be approved for the loan you want. And if you don't meet these guidelines, you probably won't get the loan because this lender can't bend the qualifying rules very much.

A second type of conventional lender requires the same down payment percentages, but is more flexible about bending the Fannie Mae guidelines. This lender will allow you to have higher ratios than is normally allowed. You may also be able to put down only 10% on investor loans. These conventional loans are sometimes called non-conforming conventional loans.

Portfolio lenders also originate loans, but unlike conventional lenders who plan to eventually sell most or all of their loans, portfolio lenders tend to keep their mortgages. This means they don't have to follow Fannie Mae guidelines. They set their own rules, and they can break them if they think you are a good credit risk. In other words, they have the flexibility to practice "make sense" underwriting when they evaluate loan applicants.

## Conventional Lenders

Most homeowners in America get a conventional loan if they don't get a FHA or VA loan. As an owner occupant you can put down as little as 3%, though you'll have to pay mortgage insurance premium (MIP) unless you put down at least 20%. Conventional fixed interest rate loans are available to investors with a minimum of 20% down. If you can qualify for a conventional loan, these loans are some of the most desirable ones because they usually offer the best fixed rates available.

Sometimes the conventional lenders will also offer community home loans to first time buyers or to households with limited incomes. These community home loans usually have very attractive interest rates and low origination costs.

Most lenders who originate conforming conventional loans do not keep them. Having your loan sold may be a minor inconvenience to you when you keep getting notices to send your mortgage payments to different lenders, but it also has a more serious consequence for you as an investor.

Since these lenders plan to immediately sell the loans they originate, they need to make sure these loans will be salable on the secondary market. This means they must follow the Fannie Mae guidelines exactly. These guidelines tend to disqualify many small investors who do not have large incomes.

## Secondary Loan Market

Overall, the existence of the secondary market for mortgages is advantageous because it allows for a free flow of money across the United States. If more money is available to loan in California than there are people who want to borrow it, the large investors who have this extra money can buy mortgages originated someplace else.

This national secondary market for loans makes it easy for local lenders to sell the mortgages they originate. The lenders can then originate more mortgages in their local markets. These lenders make money from the origination fees they charge, not from holding the mortgages and receiving the interest payments.

The big institutional investors who buy mortgages on the secondary market do not want to lose their money by buying non-performing mortgages. They want to buy loans which will have a low default rate. This means they want to buy mortgages which are as standardized as possible. A mortgage which conforms to Fannie Mae guidelines can be originated anywhere in the United States, and then be packaged with other Fannie Mae mortgages. An investor who buys a package of these mortgages knows exactly what is being bought.

If lenders don't follow the Fannie Mae guidelines, they may have trouble selling their loans immediately. Before the lender can sell non-conforming loans, the loans sometimes must be held for a period of time to season them. If the loans are current in their payments after one to two years, these loans can be sold on the secondary market just like conforming Fannie Mae conventional loans. If your lender doesn't want to hold loans to season them, then you may have to qualify using strict Fannie Mae guidelines. If you don't fit neatly into the Fannie Mae "box", your loan may not be approved.

If a conventional lender rejects your loan application because you don't meet the strict Fannie Mae guidelines, you can still approach a lender who offers non-conforming conventional loans. This lender can be more flexible because it's willing to hold the loans it originates for a short time to season them or else the lender has found an "investor" who will provide funds for loans with standards which are more flexible than Fannie Mae's. This is where a mortgage broker who works with a number of these "investors" can be very useful to you as a borrower because the mortgage broker will know about these loans.

## Portfolio Lenders

Portfolio lenders include a broad spectrum of money sources, but I'm referring to the ones commonly used to obtain first mortgages. The national biggies I'm familiar with are World Savings and Washington Mutual (these two lenders also do loans other than portfolio loans). Portfolio lenders get their name because they keep many or all of the loans they originate in their own investment portfolio of loans and/or do their own loan servicing.

These lenders are not worried about selling your loan on the secondary market. Because they keep their loans, they can make their own loan qualification requirements. If they think you are a good loan risk according to their qualifications, they will approve your loan application.

Currently, portfolio lenders are more flexible and generous in how they qualify borrowers, particularly the small investors, and this type of lender also offers the more unusual loans. Portfolio lenders are great for anyone who doesn't fit into a neat set of qualification rules. Self-employed people, limited income people (based on family income and the number of people in the family), and investors will find loans designed for their particular circumstances. Even parents who don't want to co-sign on conventional loans with their children, but who do want to help their children buy homes, are offered an alternative.

World Savings doesn't have a fixed limit on the number of loans any individual can have with them, though they will make your loan application pass through a second level of approval once the total of all the loans you have with them exceeds $750,000. Washington Mutual also has no arbitrary limits on the number of loans they will give you, but they may increase the required down payment if they feel their percentage of your real estate loans is too large. Both lenders want to minimize their risks when lending to one individual.

# Qualifying Ratios

Both conventional and portfolio lenders use what are called front end and back end ratios to determine how much they will loan to a borrower. The front end ratio, also called the housing ratio, determines the maximum mortgage payment amount they think you can handle. The back end ratio limits your total monthly debt obligations including the proposed mortgage payment.

A conventional lender following strict Fannie Mae rules will use 28% as a housing ratio. If you earn $3,000 per month gross income before taxes are taken out, the lender will multiply $3,000 by 28%. The result, $840, is the largest monthly mortgage payment the lender thinks you can handle. This amount must include principal, interest, taxes, hazard insurance, plus any mortgage insurance premiums and homeowner association dues. If the borrower intends to get a second loan in addition to the first loan, the payment for the second loan will be included as well.

You must also qualify for the loan using the back end ratio. The conventional lender will multiply your income by 36%. Using $3,000 as your gross monthly income, your back end ratio number would be $1,080. This is the largest amount of total monthly debt the lender thinks you can handle. It must include all of your "long-term" monthly debt obligations in addition to the mortgage payment on your new loan. The lender will look at such things as car payments, leases, student loans, alimony or child support and minimum monthly credit card payments, and any other revolving installment debt obligations you have.

In our example if you have a $300 car payment and a $50 student loan payment, the lender will subtract $350 from your back ratio number of $1,080 to get $730. Then the lender will compare your back end ratio number with your housing ratio number, in this example $840. Your approved loan amount is limited by the smaller of these two numbers. Since $730 is less than $840 you would be qualified for a loan with a total payment of $730 per month.

## Portfolio Lender Ratios

Portfolio lenders set their own ratios. Based on their lending experiences, they may loosen or tighten their requirements. For this next example, we will use the ratios in effect at both World Savings and Washington Mutual as of spring, 1998. Remember that these ratios can be bent for strong borrowers at the lenders' discretion.

If you apply for a loan with either of these lenders, they will use a 33% housing ratio and a 40% back end ratio. In our example of a $3,000 gross monthly income, these ratios produce $990 for the housing ratio number and $1,200 for the back end ratio number. Subtracting the same $350 in car and student loan payments from $1,200 gives us $850. Since $850 is smaller than $990, these portfolio lenders would qualify you for a maximum monthly loan payment of $850. This is still significantly higher than the $730 a strict conventional lender would establish as your maximum payment based on the same income and debts.

*NOTE:    Remember that just because you qualify for a loan based on these ratios does not mean a lender will give you a loan. Besides the ever present requirement of good credit, each lender has additional qualification requirements for the loan products they offer. Ratios are only the starting point for lenders when they qualify borrowers for a loan.*

# Rental Income

Most investors assume lenders will look at the anticipated rent for a rental property and then at the mortgage payment, and as long as there is a positive monthly cash flow, everything will be fine. It's true that when you buy an investment property the lenders will be looking at your mortgage payment for the property and the rent you will receive. But they may not credit you for the full amount of rent and they will also be looking at your personal debt situation. Even with a projected positive cash flow, the lender may not give you a loan.

# Conventional Lenders & Investment Loans

Conventional lenders will not count your full rent as income against your debt obligations. Instead they will discount your rents. Let's say you want to buy a property, 354 Primrose Drive, which will rent for $1,000 per month. Conventional lenders will give you credit for 75% of the rent, or in this example, $750. They assume that the other 25% of your rent will be spent on maintenance, advertising, and vacancy expenses.

Let's assume that your loan payment on 354 Primrose Drive will be $800. This includes principal, interest, insurance, taxes plus any homeowners association fees. Since the payment, $800, is larger than the discounted rent, $750, the lender will consider the difference, $50, as a debt which must be subtracted from your back ratio just like a car or student loan payment.

The conventional lender will look at your personal debt situation using their normal ratios. In our earlier example with a $3,000 gross monthly income, the housing ratio of 28% gave us $840 as the maximum amount for personal housing expenses and the back end ratio gave us $1,080 before being adjusted. The adjustments meant we subtracted $350 from the back end ratio number for the car and student loan payments, and now we must also subtract the negative $50 cash flow produced by the lender's discounting of the rent for your new rental property. This produces a maximum back end ratio number of $680.

Since $680 is smaller than $840, $680 is the maximum amount we can have for a total loan payment on our personal house and still qualify for the $800 payment on 354 Primrose Drive. If the total mortgage or rent payment for our personal residence exceeds $680, we won't qualify for the investment loan unless we put down additional money (a smaller loan equals a smaller loan payment) or unless we pay off some of our personal debts (to increase our back end ratio number by eliminating the car or student loan payment).

# Portfolio Lenders & Investment Loans

Portfolio lenders are more lenient when they decide how much to loan on a rental property. In addition to using higher ratios, they generally do not discount rents on the property you are buying (an exception would be if the property had more than one unit). This makes it much easier to qualify for an investment loan.

Washington Mutual and World Savings both want to see an anticipated rent which will exceed the monthly mortgage payment on the property. Since they don't discount rents on a property when it is being purchased, the positive difference between the rent amount and the mortgage payment will be added to your income to help you qualify for your personal debts!

Since 354 Primrose would rent for $1,000 per month, or $250 more than the mortgage payment of $750, these lenders would add that $250 to your monthly income of $3,000 to produce a new monthly gross income of $3,250.

*NOTE: When you buy an investment property and already have investment properties, these portfolio lenders will look at the rents from your current properties differently than the projected rent for the new property. If you get your new loan on a low documentation basis (in other words you don't provide copies of your tax returns) then the rents on your current properties will be discounted by 25%. If you get a full documentation loan, these lenders will subtract your actual costs from actual rents received as reported on your tax return. If the result is a positive number, it will help you to qualify. If it is a negative number, it will be considered part of your monthly debt obligations.*

Using World Savings' and Washington Mutual's ratios, the housing ratio of 33% would be multiplied against $3,250 instead of $3,000 since the difference between the expected rent and the mortgage payment is added to your income. This produces a housing ratio number of $1,072.50. Multiplying the back end ratio of 40% against $3,250 gives us $1,300, but then we must subtract the $350 for the car and student loan payments to produce a final back end ratio number of $950. Since $950 is smaller than $1,072.50, $950 is the maximum amount we can pay for our personal housing expenses in order to qualify for the $800 payment on 354 Primrose Drive.

*NOTE: Lenders can, and do, change their qualifying procedures at their own discretion. You must always check with local loan representatives to find out exactly how much you can qualify to borrow. Currently, neither Washington Mutual nor World Savings charges an application fee when borrowers apply for preapproval on a loan. Some lenders do charge. In either case, before you start looking for a rental property, you should get preapproved, or at least pre-qualified, by a lender. Then you will know exactly how much you can spend.*

Comparing the conventional lender against the two example portfolio lenders, we see a $270 difference in the allowable size of our personal housing costs, $680 versus $950. The portfolio lenders would allow a personal housing expense which is almost 40% higher than what a conforming conventional lender would allow.

So even though a fixed rate conventional loan may be attractive, it is easier to qualify for an adjustable rate portfolio loan. When you buy your first investment property, you may be able to qualify for a conforming conventional investor loan, but it will become increasingly more difficult to qualify for each subsequent loan.

Why? Because each new property, using our example, would count as a $50 monthly expense according to a conventional lender. Unless you have a very high income or minimal debts, your back end ratio number will quickly decrease. Eventually your back end ratio number will become too small for you to qualify for another conventional loan. At this point in time you could switch to a portfolio lender. Since the portfolio lender's back ratio is higher and the rent on the new property you are buying won't be discounted, you should still be able to get loan approvals. Indeed, for some investors who don't qualify for conventional loans, portfolio lenders will be the only choice.

## Owner Occupant Versus Investor Loans

You can count on three things when you get an investor loan instead of an owner occupant loan: your closing costs will be higher, your interest rate will be higher, and your required down payment will be higher.

Why? Because lenders perceive investors to be riskier borrowers. When either an owner occupant or an investor lets a house go into foreclosure, they each face the loss of their good credit rating and their equity. The owner occupant, however, will also lose his or her home. Lenders think homeowners will work harder to keep their homes than an investor will work to keep a rental property.

## Leap Frogging from Home to Home

If your goal is to get the best terms on your rental loans, you may want to acquire your rental properties by leap frogging. The definition of leap frogging is to buy a personal home using owner occupant financing, stay there long enough to satisfy the lender's occupancy requirement for an owner occupant, then rent that house out and buy a new personal residence. You repeat this process until you've accumulated the number of rental properties you need to achieve your financial goal. Then you concentrate on paying off your mortgages to the point where you can semi or fully retire.

Leap frogging does have its disadvantages. You may have a spouse who is willing to invest in real estate, but who is unwilling to move repeatedly. Since my husband has made it very clear on numerous occasions that he loves his house and will not move, I have been forced to use only investor financing to purchase houses since marrying Steven. The additional costs are worth it in order to maintain my husband's enthusiasm for rental houses.

Leap frogging also requires time. If you have enough money to buy more than one house, you will only be able to get an owner occupant loan on one of them. The other house or houses will either have to be purchased using investor financing or you will have to wait to buy them. You will have to live in the first house long enough to satisfy your lender's occupancy requirements before you may move into a new house using owner occupant financing again.

Lenders do realize that borrowers are sometimes forced to move and rent out a home before the occupancy time period is up. If you are transferred, the lender is most likely not going to foreclose on you or increase your interest rate, assuming that the lender notices you've moved. As long you don't tell the lender to send the payment coupons to a new address, how will the lender know? Most lenders don't pay attention until there is a problem with a loan such as late payments.

Some investors count on the lender not to pay attention. They get owner occupant financing and then immediately buy another house using owner occupant financing through a different lender. I personally do not recommend this approach, but it is done. If you are caught, you won't be sent to jail; however, the lender could call the loan due and payable. If you don't pay off your loan, the lender could then foreclose. Since a foreclosure would ruin your credit history and make future loans very hard to get, you should play by the rules or know how to get a lot of cash fast if necessary.

Both World Savings and Washington Mutual include a requirement in the deed of trust for you to live in the property for at least one year if you get owner occupied financing. Keep in mind that while you wait that year to be eligible for owner occupant financing again, housing prices may go up more than the additional cost of the investor financing you saved by waiting.

If you have enough money to buy more than one house at a time, you have to look at what's happening in your local real estate market. If the market is appreciating, it may be best to get your money invested at today's prices, even if it means paying extra for an investor loan.

Of course, if you have to save up your next down payment before you can buy another house, you can console yourself with the fact that leap frogging is custom tailored to your situation.

You will qualify for some unusual and useful loans available only to owner occupants. Plus you will be able to get fixed rate loans, something that is not always available to investors.

# Loan Terms

Should you get a standard thirty year mortgage? Or would a fifteen year mortgage be better? Maybe you should get a loan with a bi-weekly payment schedule instead of a monthly schedule. How do you decide which one is best? Sometimes you can get a better rate on a mortgage if you get a fifteen year mortgage instead of a thirty year mortgage. But the difference is usually not much, and the payments are much higher because the loan is being paid off so much faster.

These big payments are why I don't like short-term loans. Sure, you can make the bigger payment today, but what happens if you have financial troubles sometime in the future? You've thrown away your safety margin. I prefer longer loan terms.

You can and should still prepay on the mortgage despite the lower required payment amount. Most prepayment penalties won't kick in unless you prepay a substantial portion of your mortgage. As long as you stay below your loan's prepayment limit, you won't owe any penalties. Check your loan documents to be sure - don't accept a loan if you aren't allowed to prepay at least some of the principal.

If your loan has an adjustable interest rate, prepaying helps to protect you against rising interest rates as well as creating additional cash flow if interest rates stay stable. For a fixed rate mortgage you are building equity and shortening the term of the loan. If you get in a tight spot financially, you can always stop making prepayments for a while. When you get back on your feet you can start prepaying again. This flexibility in how much you pay on your thirty year mortgages will make it easier to be a long-term investor.

# Forty Year Mortgages

Some lenders, including World Savings and Washington Mutual, will give owner occupants a forty year mortgage instead of a thirty year mortgage (you have to ask for one). For example, a loan for $100,000 at 7.5% interest over thirty years would have a principal and interest payment of $699.21 per month. If you lengthened the loan term from thirty years to forty years, the principal and interest payment would drop to $658.07.

The payment difference is only $41.14 per month, or $493.68 per year, but if you leap frog from one property to the next, you could get this extra leeway on several loans. Multiplying $493.68 by five properties would be $2,468.40 per year.

Personally, I've never gotten a forty year mortgage, but it's another technique you can use to lower your risk as an investor by reducing your required monthly payment amounts. It also may make the difference between qualifying for the next loan or not because it reduces your monthly debt payments.

# Bi-Weekly Mortgage Payments

When you compare bi-weekly payment mortgages against monthly payment mortgages, you should realize that the only net difference is you will make one additional principal and interest payment per year with the bi-weekly payment mortgage. There is nothing to stop you from doing this with a typical monthly mortgage. You can either make an extra principal and interest payment each year, or you can divide that payment by twelve and add that amount to your monthly payments. The effect is the same as the bi-weekly mortgage except that if you run into financial tough times, you can stop making the extra payments on the monthly mortgage.

For someone who has the discipline to pre-pay, I believe a bi-weekly mortgage is not a good choice. You will be sacrificing financial flexibility in exchange for a twenty-three year mortgage. I believe you should retain the ability to decide whether or not to prepay based on your year-to-year financial situation instead of signing up for a bi-weekly mortgage. You can still reduce your mortgage term by pre-paying, but you will have room to maneuver financially just in case.

# Prepayment Penalties

Prepayment penalties can come in many different forms. Sometimes you are limited as to the percentage of your loan balance you are allowed to pay off in any one year. Sometimes you will owe a penalty if you pay off your entire loan too fast. For example, if your loan has a three year prepayment penalty, and you sell the house after owning it only two years, you will owe a penalty which may equal thousands of dollars.

Always ask about prepayment penalties when you are shopping for a loan. Sometimes lenders will waive any prepayment penalties if you pay an additional amount in closing costs. If you are buying a fixer upper that you plan to improve and then sell quickly, you may be willing to pay an extra point in order to get a loan without a prepayment penalty.

If, on the other hand, you plan to own the house for at least as long as the prepayment penalty period, you will probably want to get the cheaper loan. Sometimes lenders will offer you ways to avoid paying the prepayment penalty even if you do sell the house within the penalty period.

World Savings, for example, does have prepayment penalties, but they will waive a prepayment penalty if you get another loan through them within six months of paying off the old loan. They will also waive the penalty if the buyer of your house gets a loan through them or assumes the old loan. So usually you can avoid prepayment penalties as long as you are paying attention and do something to make the lender happy.

# Chapter Six

# Adjustable Rate Mortgages

Adjustable rate mortgages scare a lot of people. They, or someone they knew, had an adjustable rate loan, and the interest rate kept shooting up the first few years. They decided that adjustable rate mortgages are awfully risky.

Adjustable rate mortgages do have some inherent risks, but both you and the lender can do a lot to minimize them. Lenders hate foreclosing on properties, and they've learned since the early days of adjustable rate mortgages how to reduce the chances of getting back properties instead of loan payments. This chapter will discuss the safeguards that are now built into most adjustable rate mortgages.

It's important for you to understand exactly how adjustable rate mortgages work so you can use them to your advantage. I'm going to tell you what a teaser rate is, the meaning of the words index and margin, what happens when you prepay an adjustable rate mortgage compared to a fixed rate mortgage, and how the different types of caps on your loan's adjustable interest rate function. When you know how to use them, adjustable rate mortgages have a valuable place in an investor's strategy.

Despite my hesitation when I obtained my first adjustable rate mortgage, I've grown to love this type of loan. Adjustable rate mortgages have allowed me to semi-retire years earlier than

I could have with fixed rate investor loans. But before we talk about the different types of adjustable rate mortgages and how the interest rates are calculated, I'm going to tell you the one absolute rule I have for adjustable rate mortgages; you must prepay them. This will help to protect you against rising interest rates.

# How Much to Prepay

I don't have a special formula. I pick a number between what I have to pay each month and the amount I'm receiving in rent. I like to pay enough extra each month so that any small upward adjustments in the interest rate won't bring the required payment anywhere close to what I'm already used to paying.

For example, my monthly payment for principal and interest for one Colorado house with an adjustable rate mortgage was $766. This payment kept me on a thirty year amortization schedule. I received $1,135 per month in rent and I paid the mortgage company $850. Since $850 was well above $766, the small monthly changes in the interest rate never brought my payment close to the amount I was used to paying. Also, because there was a lot of room between the $850 I paid and the $1,135 I received in rent, I didn't worry about interest rate increases. I could easily pay even more each month if it became necessary.

Did I ever pay less than $850? Sometimes. My minimum required payment at that time was actually $704 instead of $766. Whenever I had to tap into my emergency fund to pay for a big expense on one of my properties such as a new furnace or roof, I wanted to replenish my emergency fund as soon as possible. This meant I might pay only the minimum required payments for each of my adjustable rate mortgages for the next month or two. I would take the extra cash flow and deposit it into my emergency fund. Once I reached my minimum desired emergency fund balance, I would go back to my standard prepayment schedule.

I may decide to increase my prepayments someday as my rents continue to go up, but since I'm only semi-retired, that won't happen for awhile. Since I would like to be completely financially independent, I would prefer to use any extra income for personal living expenses instead of increasing my prepayment amounts. The only exception would be if interest rates started to rise. Then it may make sense to protect myself by prepaying more and continuing to work part-time.

## Adjustable Interest Rates

When you shop for loans you'll discover that adjustable interest rates are generally lower than fixed interest rates. This difference in rates is insurance for the lender. On a fixed rate loan, the lender is concerned about interest rates rising. Since the lender won't be able to raise the rate on the fixed rate loan, the lender has the potential to lose money in the future. To compensate for this risk, the lender charges a higher fixed rate. If rates do rise, the lender will have been collecting a higher amount of interest ahead of time. If rates don't rise, the lender will make additional money.

With an adjustable rate mortgage the lender is protected if interest rates go up; therefore the lender will generally offer a lower starting interest rate on an adjustable rate mortgage. If interest rates rise, the borrower will have to make bigger payments to the lender. Prepaying on an adjustable rate mortgage will decrease the principal balance of your loan. The smaller your loan balance becomes, the less an increase in interest rates will affect you.

## Teaser Rates

Many adjustable rate mortgages come with teaser rates. The interest rates are abnormally low in the beginning and then adjust upward. If you didn't expect and plan for these adjustments, you could find yourself in a bad position. You always need to find out the current fully indexed rate when you shop for an adjustable rate mortgage. The fully indexed rate is the interest rate you would be paying if you had been holding the mortgage long enough to be past any below market teaser rates.

The loan officer may not understand what you mean when you ask for the fully indexed rate. He or she may keep telling you about the teaser rate, explaining that the fully indexed rate can't be determined until you've had the loan long enough for the rate to adjust to future market conditions. Since no one can foretell the future, they can't tell you the fully indexed rate.

Fine. Tell the loan officer you realize you won't have to pay the fully indexed rate right away. You know it's impossible to predict the future, so of course they can't tell you what the fully indexed rate will be in two years. But they can tell you what the fully indexed rate would be today assuming you had this loan for the past five years. If the loan officer still doesn't know what you're asking for, you can figure it out for yourself.

## Index and Margin

A fully indexed rate is the index plus the margin. The index changes over time and it is what causes your interest rate to change along with it. Many conventional loans use the treasury bill rates as their index. Portfolio lenders frequently use an index such as the COFI, the cost of funds index. (The COFI index is calculated each month by averaging the interest rates being paid on all the savings and checking accounts in the eleventh district of the federal banking system plus the interest rates being paid on certificates of deposit.) Ask the lender to tell you what index is used by the loan you are considering.

Next find out what the margin is for this loan. The margin represents the lender's gross profit margin before subtracting expenses. If the COFI index is at 4.651 and the lender's margin for an owner occupant loan is 2.5, your fully indexed loan rate will equal these two numbers added together, or 7.151%. The margin for an investor will be higher, perhaps 2.8 instead of 2.5, making the investor interest rate 7.451%.

Once you get your loan your margin will remain constant unless otherwise specified in your deed of trust. However, lenders do change the margins they charge for new loans depending upon market conditions. You may get a COFI loan with a margin of 2.6% this year, but next year when you buy another house using another COFI loan, the bank may have increased or reduced its margin. The index will be the same for the two loans since they are both tied to the COFI index, but since the margin is different, you'll have two different interest rates.

I have six adjustable rate mortgages. One is linked to the treasury bill index and the rest are linked to the COFI index. Only two of my loans have the same interest rate. Depending on when I bought my houses, the lenders were offering different margins. When you are considering refinancing you may want to ask if a lender is about to raise or lower its margin. You may decide to hurry up or slow down your loan application depending on what you are told.

I personally like loans tied to the COFI index. Since it is based partly on interest rates paid on certificates of deposit, it tends not to change quickly. Most people who have certificates of deposit want to avoid early withdrawal penalties. Even when interest rates are rising they usually wait until their certificates of deposits mature before they pull out their money to reinvest. So when interest rates increase the COFI lags behind while people wait to roll over their certificates of deposit.

If you have an adjustable rate mortgage which uses the COFI as its index, your loan's interest rate will climb more slowly than will interest rates on adjustable rate mortgages which are tied to more volatile indexes. On the downside your loan's interest rate will also fall more slowly when interest rates go back down. I consider this a fair trade off. The more slowly my loan interest rates change, the easier it is for me to adjust my investment plans accordingly.

# Comparing Adjustable Rate Mortgages

Teaser rates make it hard to compare different adjustable rate mortgages. A teaser rate may be only 4% the first six months you have the loan, but then the terms of your loan agreement may allow it to go up a maximum of two points every six months until you reach the fully indexed rate. Assuming the fully indexed homeowner rate is 7.151, you'll pay the 4% teaser rate for the first six months, 6% for the next six months, and then 7.151% thereafter, assuming the index rate hasn't changed between now and then. How do you compare this against a loan that starts out fully indexed at 6.955%?

There is no foolproof method to pick the loan with the best adjustable rate in a situation like this, but you should consider several factors. First, you can compare the fully indexed rates. It is possible that one loan may have a great teaser rate, but its fully indexed rate is much higher than the loan with no teaser rate. In this case you would choose the loan with the lower fully indexed rate if you planned to own the property for a significant length of time.

On the other hand perhaps both loans have the same or close to the same fully indexed rates. Then you should take advantage of the temporary low teaser rate loan while you wait for its interest rate to become fully indexed.This is assuming that the closing costs are comparable.

Second, you should consider how long you plan to own a given property. If you hope to fix up a property and sell it quickly for a profit, you may want the loan with the teaser rate, even if its fully indexed rate is higher than for other adjustable rate mortgages. Why pay more interest now when you don't plan to own the property by the time the interest rate has a chance to increase?

Some lenders offer loans with identical fully indexed rates. In order to get the teaser rate you must pay higher closing costs. The money you'll be saving while the teaser rate is in effect will be spent instead on higher origination fees. Usually when you compare the total costs, the loan costs balance out to be equal.

# Interest Rate Caps

Comparing the fully indexed rates of two different loans is important, but you should also look at the caps for each loan. A cap is a maximum interest rate. Most adjustable rate mortgages have two caps, an annual interest or payment cap and a lifetime cap.

The annual cap comes in many versions. The most common cap is an interest cap which allows the lender to raise the interest rate on your loan on an annual or sometimes bi-annual basis. The cap is the maximum amount your interest rate can increase. Many loans have caps which allow your interest rate to increase by only one or two percent with each adjustment, for example from 6% to 7%.

Other loans have payment caps instead of interest rate caps. This type of loan can raise your principal and interest payment by a certain percentage of the payment itself, for example 7.5%. As an example let's say your principal and interest payment is $1,000. The lender could increase your required payment by 7.5% of $1,000, or up to $1,075.

Sometimes caps are true caps and sometimes they are not. What I call a true cap works as follows. When your rate adjusts, you owe a certain interest rate on your loan balance and that's all you must pay. Other caps may limit your required payment, but not the interest rate you are charged. If the required payment isn't large enough to cover the increased interest, the lender adds this difference to your loan balance. These types of loans are called negative amortization loans.

For example, let's say that your loan payment is $1,000. The index rate your loan is tied to has gone up and therefore so has the interest rate on your loan. If your loan has a 7.5% payment cap, the lender can only increase your required payment to $1,075. But let's say this is not enough of an increase to pay for the higher interest charges. Since the lender can't increase your required payment again until the next adjustment time, the lender takes whatever interest charges are not covered by the new payment and adds this amount to your loan balance.

This doesn't necessarily mean that your loan balance will increase because some of your required payment pays off principal. Let's say that $200 of your $1,075 payment is going to principal, and your unpaid interest each month is $35. If your loan balance was $120,000, then the lender would subtract the principal payment and add the unpaid interest.

| | |
|---|---|
| **Principal portion of mortgage payment** | **$200** |
| **Unpaid interest** | **$35** |
| **Loan balance** | **$120,000** |
| **New loan balance after receiving payment** ($120,000 - $200 + $35) | **$119,835** |

You won't be paying off your loan as quickly because some of your monthly principal payments will be canceled out by the unpaid interest. In worst case scenarios it could mean your loan amount actually starts to increase because your payments toward principal are less than the unpaid interest.

This type of loan may sound awful, but don't panic and swear you would never get a negative amortization loan. You always have the option to pay the unpaid interest. The lender will tell you the required payment you must make in order to keep your loan in good standing, and you will also be told how much extra you should pay if you want to keep your loan on a regular thirty year amortization basis. Since you should be prepaying on your adjustable rate mortgages every month anyway, this may not be a problem for you.

When you have a choice it is best to get a loan where the lender swallows the negative amounts when interest rates are rising. These loans are usually the conventional loans. Most portfolio loans are negative amortization loans.

Remember that lenders don't want to foreclose on their loans. By limiting how much you must pay when interest rates go up and adding the unpaid interest to your loan balance, they are giving you a mini-loan without you having to apply for it. Why should you worry about your loan balance increasing as long as your property is appreciating in value at a faster rate? Plus the limitation on your required payment increase gives you time to slowly raise your rents to cover your new higher payment amounts.

## Lifetime Caps

The lifetime cap is the maximum your interest rate can ever be. This cap is almost always a true cap. That means that if interest rates exceed your lifetime cap, you don't have to pay the difference even on portfolio loans. No unpaid interest above the cap interest rate is added to your principal balance. No matter how high rates go, the lifetime cap interest rate is the worst case scenario for you even if you have a negative amortization loan.

I think you should only get loans which do have a true lifetime interest cap. You can use the worst case interest scenario when you are looking at loans. Ask the lender to tell you what your principal and interest payment would be based on the full loan amount and the lifetime cap rate. This payment plus taxes and insurance will almost always exceed the anticipated rent, but not by much. Your potential negative cash flow will probably be less than two hundred dollars on a property in the $150,000 price range with 20% down.

This worst case scenario assumes that rates shoot up instantly before you have a chance to pay down your loan. If you're looking at an adjustable rate mortgage which is tied to the Treasury bill rate as its index, ask yourself how high and how fast you think the Federal Reserve will let rates increase. No matter how fast, it won't produce an interest rate equal to your lifetime cap rate instantaneously. You will have time to adjust.

If you're looking at an adjustable rate mortgage which is tied to the COFI index, ask yourself how fast you think the interest rates paid on savings and checking accounts are going to rise. If your margin is 2.5 and your lifetime interest rate cap is 12.5%, this means the COFI index would have to be 10 before you hit the maximum interest rate.

How soon do you think savings accounts will be paying 8%, or certificates of deposit will be paying 12%? These are the types of interest rates you would probably see before the COFI index became 10 or higher. It happened in the eighties. Do you think it will happen again? How fast do you think it could happen?

## Worst Case Scenario

Even in the hypothetical worst case scenario of instantly skyrocketing interest rates you would probably still make a profit. Though your cash flow rate of return might be negative, you would still be paying down the principal balance of your loan, receiving tax benefits from depreciation, and possibly experiencing appreciation.

## Why I'm Not Afraid of Adjustable Rate Mortgages

I figure that if interest rates go up, it will be harder for home buyers to qualify for loans. That means they will be forced to rent instead. High interest rates will also stop many investors from purchasing properties because their lifetime caps will be set at 15% or higher on new loans. So with more demand for rentals and with a limited supply available, I think I'll be able to raise my rents enough so I won't have a negative cash flow. Plus, since I put down at least 20% when I buy houses, my cash flows are large enough to accommodate significant payment increases even if I can't raise my rents immediately.

My philosophy is to buy and hold real estate. As long as I put down enough money, prepay on my adjustable rate mortgages, and raise my rents as the market rises, I think I'll be able to weather the ups and downs of the real estate market including changes in the interest rates on my loans.

The interest rates on my adjustable mortgages have jiggled a little bit up and a little bit down, but basically they've stayed at about 7.7%. In the meantime I've been prepaying my mortgages and watching my required monthly mortgage payments get smaller every year.

When I prepay on my fixed mortgages I don't get the same positive feedback. Sure, I'm reducing the length of my fixed mortgages from thirty years down to nineteen years based on the amount I'm prepaying, but who wants to wait that long for a mortgage payment to finally disappear?

Psychologically it's been a lot less fun to prepay on my fixed mortgages because my payments always stay the same. Unless I can raise my rents, my cash flow doesn't improve each year. Of course, neither will it have a chance to decrease due to rising interest rates, but I would rather take that risk in exchange for the chance to see my income rise more quickly.

Prepaying on my adjustable rate mortgages allowed me to semi-retire in my early thirties. I let my real estate license go inactive and I work occasional part-time jobs to earn the difference between my rental income and my bills. I'm still prepaying on my mortgages so even as I enjoy my semi-retirement, my required payments will continue to drop each year as long as interest rates stay stable. Without having to work full-time I'm enjoying a standard of living which is rising faster than inflation.

You can enjoy mortgage payments which get smaller, too, if you are willing to take the risk of having adjustable rate mortgages and you faithfully prepay extra money every month. The opportunity to be semi-retired in only five to ten years is amazing. It's a goal that's close enough to be real, something you can almost touch.

Even after you semi-retire, your net worth and income will continue to increase, even when all you're doing is taking care of your rentals and earning some extra money on the side to cover expenses until you can fully retire. Slowly but surely your tenants will be paying off your mortgages and your rents will continue to rise over a span of years.

Can you imagine working only part-time at jobs you like while you wait for your income to double or triple at some point in the future when your mortgages are paid off? And in the meantime the inflation numbers in the newspaper don't scare you because your rents, and therefore your income, is rising. Even if you prefer fixed mortgages, the advantages of adjustable rate mortgages make it worthwhile to consider having both types of loans. Adjustable rate mortgages bring an early semi-retirement within reach.

## Prepay Your Adjustable Rate Mortgages

The key is to prepay your adjustable rate mortgages. Yes, it's tempting to take your cash flow and save it all toward the down payment on your next house. And as long as interest rates don't rise substantially, you'll be okay and you'll get rich faster than the person who is more cautious. Why? Because you'll own more houses sooner since your money is going toward down payments instead of to prepayments.

But the downside is what happens if interest rates do rise. Will you be able to make your mortgage payments if your payment amounts rise and you haven't been prepaying? Deciding how much risk you are willing to tolerate is up to you, but I'd rather be able to keep what I have than gamble it all on having even more. I strongly recommend prepaying your loans even if it means slowing down your acquisition program.

Of course prepaying your loans doesn't mean you have to semi-retire before you pay them off. You can keep prepaying and get rid of those thirty year mortgages as fast as you can and then fully retire.

Even if you plan to keep working until you've paid off your loans entirely, the real world may interfere. You may get laid-off from your job or you may experience health problems that force you to stop working. Perhaps you will want to spend more time with an aging family member. If you've been prepaying on your adjustable rate mortgages, and interest rates have stayed reasonable, you'll have options not available to those who have partially paid-off their fixed rate mortgages.

True, those who have fixed rate mortgages could refinance in order to make the payments smaller, but this may pose a couple of problems. It costs money in the form of the closing costs for a new loan on each property that you refinance. And if your need for money is due to financial trouble in your life, you may discover that lenders aren't willing to give you new loans. You may be forced to sell a property to get the money you need for living expenses while you reorganize your life. Fixed rate mortgages just aren't as flexible as adjustable rate mortgages.

# Chapter Seven

# A Selection of Loans

A wonderful smorgasbord of loan products is available in the United States. The majority of lenders and real estate agents are very familiar with FHA loans, VA loans, and conventional loans. Since information on these loans is widely available, this chapter concentrates instead on the variety of loans offered by the portfolio lenders.

These loans are not familiar to most people, even real estate professionals. Some of the loans I'm about to describe are offered to investors, but some are only available to owner occupants. Keep in mind that most of these loans are adjustable rate mortgages unless I indicate otherwise.

Even if some of these loans won't work for you, they may work for someone you know, or one of them may be perfect for you in the future. The variety of loans available makes it possible for almost anyone with good credit, or even not-so-good credit, to borrow money. After reading this chapter, you'll know about more types of loans than do many real estate agents.

While any bank can be a portfolio lender if its loan officers decide to lend money to someone and keep the loan in the bank's portfolio, these loans are uncommon and are awarded on a case-by-case basis. If you have a strong relationship with your bank, you may be able to obtain one of these individualized portfolio loans. Usually, though, portfolio loans will come from one of the big national savings and loans who specialize in this type of loan.

Quite a bit of consolidation of portfolio lenders has occurred in the past couple of years. Washington Mutual has purchased three large portfolio lenders, American Savings, Great Western and Home Savings. All of these companies will be operating under the name of Washington Mutual. The other large national portfolio lender with which I'm familiar is World Savings. There are probably other portfolio lenders across the country. To locate them ask a number of real estate agents in your area if they know of portfolio lenders who serve your state.

Many of the loan products offered by World Savings and Washington Mutual are very similar, but differences do exist. In addition to charging different margins on their adjustable rate loans (margins change occasionally), these lenders also have different restrictions on what types of properties they consider acceptable as collateral.

World Savings, for example, doesn't do loans on mixed use properties. So if you decide to buy a condominium in a building that also has office spaces, World Savings may not be able to help you, but Washington Mutual, as of spring 1998, would be interested in taking a look at your application.

Since lenders can change, add or eliminate loan programs at their discretion, the loans described in this chapter may change. But most of these loan products have been available for years and will continue to be offered for the foreseeable future. Check with your local loan representatives for the latest information on loan availability and requirements.

## The 100% Loan (Or How Not to Co-sign)

This loan is offered by both Washington Mutual and World Savings. It can be a fabulous loan for two types of people - those who want to help a friend or relative to buy a personal residence, and those who need that help. You may find yourself in either of these positions.

The most common way to assist a weak borrower obtain a loan is for someone to co-sign on the loan, but this ties up the co-signer's credit since she or he also becomes liable for the full monthly payment. This makes it more difficult for the co-signor to qualify for other loans. And if the borrower doesn't pay the mortgage payments, the co-signor's good credit may be ruined.

If the potential co-signer doesn't want to tie up his or her credit or risk it being damaged, he or she could still help the weak borrower by giving the borrower a large sum of money to use as a down payment. Loans called low documentation loans are available which will look at a borrower's credit but not at the borrower's income if the down payment is large enough.

The problem here is obvious. It's one thing to help a borrower, but another matter entirely to give the borrower twenty thousand dollars. Also lenders may not be happy that the down payment is a gift instead of the borrower's own funds.

The 100% loan solves these problems, though it has a catch. World Savings or Washington Mutual will lend 100% of the purchase price of a home to a borrower. Instead of a down payment they will expect a sponsor to put 20% of the purchase price into certificates of deposit to be held by the lender as collateral in addition to the house itself. (As an example of changing loan terms, World Savings recently required an amount equal to 25% of the purchase price to be held as collateral instead of 20%.)

The sponsor does not co-sign the loan with the borrower and the sponsor retains ownership of the certificates of deposit. The sponsor can choose to invest his or her money in any type of certificate of deposit, from a three month certificate to a six year certificate. The sponsor will receive the monthly interest earned on the certificates of deposit.

The risk for the sponsor is that the borrower will not make the loan payments. The lender will notify the sponsor if payments become delinquent. If the payments are not brought current the lender may foreclose and the sponsor will lose the money held as collateral. But even if this happens, since the sponsor did not co-sign on the loan, the sponsor's credit will not be affected.

This type of loan also provides the sponsor with several other advantages. The sponsor's ability to borrow is not reduced by the new mortgage because he or she is not co-signing the loan. This makes it easier for the sponsor to still qualify for other loans. Also, since the money in the secured certificates of deposit is not given to the borrower, it still belongs to the sponsor. As such, it remains in the sponsor's estate in the case of death to be divided in whatever manner the sponsor wants among his or her heirs (though it will remain pledged as collateral). This can be very advantageous when a parent wants to help one child without causing resentment in the other children.

It is not even necessary for the sponsor to risk the full 20% of the purchase price required for the collateral. If the borrower puts down some money, then the sponsor only needs to put the difference into the secured certificates of deposit. For example, if the borrower puts down 5%, then the sponsor will need to put 15% into the secured certificates of deposit.

The funds in the certificates of deposit are not tied up forever. As soon as the equity in the property reaches 20%, either the borrower or the sponsor can pay for an appraisal to prove this. If the appraisal shows that the loan has been reduced to 80% or less of the property value, the secured certificates of deposit are released. This reduction of the loan-to-value ratio to 80% is accomplished through a combination of principal paydown on the loan balance and appreciation of the property.

At this time, this loan product is offered only to owner occupants, but it can be great for the younger investor who has a parent or grandparent who would like to help him or her to buy a personal residence. And it can be just as advantageous for the parent who hates the idea of co-signing. You can help your kid buy a house without messing up your ability to qualify for investment loans!

# Low Documentation Loans

Low documentation loans (low doc loans) or no income veri-fication loans are offered both to investors and to owner occu-pants, though the investor loan will have a higher margin and a larger required down payment. Both margins and down payment minimums may change depending on market conditions. As of spring, 1998, the down payment for either a Washington Mutual or World Savings low doc owner occupant loan was 20%. For investors the down payment was 30%.

Low documentation loans are some of the easiest loans to get. They are ideally suited for self-employed people who are successfully utilizing the tax system to reduce their reported in-come to next to nothing. It's also a great loan for those people who have an erratic employment history. With this type of loan, however, you must have sparkling credit, and you must show proof of your employment. If you have a small ding on your credit history you may still qualify for a low documentation loan, but the required down payment may be increased.

An example of someone who used this loan to his advan-tage was a student who wanted to sell his townhouse and buy a house closer to the school he attended. As a student working part-time evenings and weekends, his income was just over $10,000 per year. The house he wanted to buy cost $122,000. Normally he would never have been able to qualify for the loan until after he had graduated and found a full-time job.

But this student had quite a bit of equity in his townhouse, enough so that when he sold it, he had the required down pay-ment on the house. Since low documentation loans don't require the lender to verify a borrower's income, he told them he made the amount necessary to qualify for the loan. The lender did not ask to see his income tax returns because lenders don't verify income for low documentation loans. This student's loan was approved with a minimum of fuss.

However, most low doc lenders will want to know where a borrower is getting the down payment. It's okay to borrow against your stocks, get a second mortgage from a friend against a rental property you own, or to pull the money out of savings. World Savings will also allow it to be a gift for both owner occupied and investor loans, while Washington Mutual will allow a portion of it to be a gift.

In addition you will need to provide proof of your employment. If you say you are an author, you may need to produce a copy of your book or a portfolio of your published magazine articles. If you are a real estate agent or professional masseuse, you'll need to provide a copy of your license. The lender will help you to determine what will serve as adequate proof.

# Limited Income Loans

Another loan that works well for the self-employed who are masters at reducing their taxable income is the limited income loan offered at World Savings. This loan also works for those borrowers whose incomes truly are low, especially if they have large families. Elderly people who want to reduce their monthly mortgage payment can be ideal candidates to refinance with this program.

This loan can be used as purchase money when you first buy a property, or as refinancing money. The closing costs charged by the lender total only $500, though additional closing costs may be charged by other parties such as the title company who handles the closing.

This loan is unusual even among portfolio loans because it has a fixed rate with very low closing costs. If you can qualify for it, it may well be the best loan available for owner occupants. Unfortunately, this fabulous loan is not available to investors, though an owner occupant may use it to purchase a duplex.

You'll have to check with World Savings to see if your income falls under the maximum allowed for your geographical area. Your maximum allowed income will also vary depending on the number of people in your household. World Savings can be very broad in its interpretation of household members, but everybody's income will have to be included. Keep this loan in mind for older folks. Since this loan is also available for refinancing, this could be a perfect loan for retired people who would like to refinance to lower their mortgage payment.

## 25% and 20% Down Investor Loans

The standard World Savings investor loan requires full documentation of your income and debts, and you must put 25% down. You must qualify to handle your own personal home mortgage payment and other monthly debts and the rental property must produce a cash flow after subtracting your anticipated monthly payments from the anticipated rent. Washington Mutual requires 20% down instead of 25%.

In order to put down only 20% with World Savings, you must ask for them to make an exception. As long as you are a strong borrower and the house is the type which would be easy to sell (standard floorplan in a good location), you will probably be told yes.

Though investor loans with down payments as low as 10% are currently available for some non-conforming conventional loans, the reason you may want a portfolio loan are the more generous front and back end ratios of the portfolio lenders. These ratios make it easier to qualify for a loan. Also, putting 20-25% down should keep the mortgage payment low enough to produce a decent cash flow situation. You can use this cash flow to prepay on your mortgage with money left over to cover maintenance costs plus some savings. The future amount of cash flow will depend on whether or not interest rates stay low and if you've been prepaying.

If the starting interest rate on your investor adjustable rate loan is under 8%, then your PITI (principal, interest, taxes and insurance) payment hopefully will be no more than 75% of your anticipated monthly rent. For example, if my payment was going to be $900, I'd like to see a rent of at least $1,200. Preferably your rent should be even higher. You need this spread between your first mortgage payment and the rent to provide a good cash flow rate of return on your invested money as well as to give you financial room to adjust in case interest rates go up or rents go down.

# The 80-10-10 or 80-15-5 Loan

It's much easier to get a non-FHA or VA loan with a low down payment than it used to be. With the creation of MIP (mortgage insurance premium), lenders can make loans with less than 20% down without taking undue risk. If a borrower defaults on the loan, the mortgage insurance company will either buy the property from the lender at the lender's cost, or else pay the lender money to defray any or some losses when the lender obtains control of the property and has to sell it.

This mortgage insurance is not the same as the type sold to homeowners by insurance agents which quarantees to pay off your mortgage if you die. This insurance is entirely for the lender's benefit, but you are the one who will pay for it. You shouldn't complain, though, because otherwise you would have to put down much more money in order to qualify for a loan.

If you don't like the idea of paying mortgage insurance payments, you have two options. You can put down 20% of the purchase price, or you can get two loans, one for 80% and a seoncd for either 10% or 15% of the purchase price. The final 10% or 5% is your down payment.

· Many lenders offer to make these second loans. Not surprisingly, they will charge you a higher interest rate than you pay on your first mortgage. In addition the loan term will generally be shorter than the first mortgage. The combination of these two factors can make the second mortgage payment fairly high. But unlike the mortgage insurance payments, the interest on the second will be tax deductible when you are buying a house as your personal home. The key question is whether it will cost less for you to pay the MIP or to have a second mortgage at the higher interest rate.

You have to do the numbers and compare your monthly payments. More precisely, you can ask your lender on the first mortgage to do the numbers for you. Loan officers can tell you who offers these second purchase money loans, and what the terms are. This is another good time to shop around.

Some lenders like World Savings have made arrangements with a second purchase money source to allow World Savings to provide the first and second purchase money loans as a package deal. You make one loan application instead of two. The second mortgage source World Savings is currently working with is MBNA. MBNA also offers a thirty year amortization on its second mortgages which makes the payments on the second loan quite reasonable.

If the first mortgage lender has to direct you elsewhere for your second mortgage because they don't do them in-house, look for a lender who offers a thirty year amortization. Verify that you are allowed to prepay. It makes sense to concentrate all of your prepaying into the second mortgage because it will be such a small note. In a few years you'll be able to pay it off and have your total monthly payments drop in a very satisfactory way.

# Foreign Nationals

Sometimes it can be difficult for foreign nationals to get loans. Washington Mutual offers adjustable rate mortgages to foreign nationals with 25% down while World Savings requires 35% down. If the foreign national has a green card, World Savings requires a down payment of 30%.

# Fixed Rate Investor Portfolio Loan

Both Washington Mutual and World Savings offer fixed loan products for investors though the interest rate may be higher than for conventional fixed loans. If you can't qualify for a fixed rate conventional mortgage, but you hate the idea of an adjustable rate mortgage, this loan may be your best choice. The portfolio ratios may make the difference in being approved or not.

# Construction/Permanent Financing

Washington Mutual offers a construction loan which becomes permanent financing after the building is completed. The minimum down payment is 20% for owner occupants. Washington Mutual also offers this loan to builders who are constructing a number of homes.

# Stacked Units

Both World Savings and Washington Mutual will loan on townhouses and condominiums, but they have a few restrictions. First, they both require a 50% owner occupancy ratio. For example, if there are 100 units, a minimum of 50 need to be owned by owner occupants. (This information can be obtained from the homeowners association.)

Also lenders may not offer loans on stacked units in some areas. World Savings will only loan on buildings with a maximum of three units stacked on top of each other in the Denver area, but will happily do loans for much taller condominium buildings in Florida. In addition, World Savings won't make loans on units which used to be apartments before being converted to condominiums. Washington Mutual does not have this restriction on converted units and will also loan on buildings without a limit on the number of stacked units.

## Convertible Loans

World Savings offers loans which start out as adjustable rate mortgages, but later they can be converted to fixed rate mortgages between months thirteen and seventy-two. The fixed rates are not as attractive as those offered by conventional lenders, but this loan may be your best choice if you can only qualify for an adjustable rate mortgage, but you really want a fixed rate.

After waiting a year you can convert your mortgage without requalifying and get that fixed rate. You will have paid smaller closing costs by starting with an adjustable rate mortgage than you would had to pay for a fixed rate portfolio loan. This loan is only offered to owner occupants.

## Fixer Upper Loan

Imagine this scenario: You buy a house for a great price, fix it up so it's worth a lot more, and then want to refinance out some of your new equity so you can buy another house. In the past lenders would refuse to give you a new loan until you had owned the property for a length of time, frequently a year. In the meantime your equity was trapped in the property.

Washington Mutual has recently decided to drop this holding, or seasoning requirement. Now they will refinance your property based on its appraised value even if you recently purchased the property for a lot less. Even if you did nothing to fix the property up, you simply bought it for a great price, that's fine with them. Your original purchase price and how long you've owned the property doesn't matter to them. All they want to know is the current appraised value.

## Bankruptcy, Foreclosure and Other Credit Problems

Portfolio lenders are much more flexible about credit problems such as a bankruptcy or foreclosure than are conventional lenders. Once two years have passed since either of these financial disasters took place, both World Savings and Washington Mutual will be happy to look at a loan applicant who experienced either of them. As long as the applicant has been financially responsible during the intervening two year period the chances are good that she or he can get a loan.

Sometimes credit problems are more general, resulting from such things as late payments and bounced checks. This means that an applicant can no longer qualify for "A" rates, but some conventional lenders and Washington Mutual offer "B" and "C" rates. These rates are higher, of course, than "A" rates, but at least it is possible to get a loan. If the borrower later improves his or her credit, it may be possible to refinance and get a better interest rate at that time.

## Second Loans on Investment Properties

When you buy a property you are getting a purchase money loan. Later when you decide to refinance the property you will be getting a refinancing loan. What is the difference between these two types of loans? The most important difference is the loan-to-value ratio. If a lender would loan up to 80% of the purchase price of a property to an investor, that same investor could only get a loan up to 70% of the appraised value when doing a refinance.

This makes it difficult to get equity out of an investment property without selling it. The solution can be a second loan. Though many lenders will only lend up to a total of 70% loan-to-value including the second, a reasonable number of lenders will loan up to an 80% loan-to-value. Another advantage to getting a second instead of a new first mortgage is lower closing costs. Instead of paying an origination fee for a large loan, you pay an origination fee on a much smaller second.

Finding a lender who offers good terms on investment property seconds requires making a number of phone calls. Your best bets will be the small local banks instead of the large regional or national banks. In the spring of 1998 I was quoted an amazing variety of terms, from great to financially prohibitive.

When you make your calls you'll want to ask the following questions. What is the interest rate? Is it fixed or adjustable? Or is it fixed for a number of years and then it becomes adjustable? Over how many years is it amortized? What are the closing costs? Besides origination fees, make sure to ask about loan processing fees and any title insurance requirements. Will you have to pay for an appraisal on the property or will the lender accept documentation on comparable sales in the neighborhood?

Some lenders I talked with made their loans economically unattractive by their demands for appraisals and title insurance. Paying $300 for an appraisal and $700 for brand new title insurance plus other closing costs would make getting a second too expensive as far as I was concerned.

But other lenders were more reasonable. One bank even had total closing costs which were less than $250 on a proposed second for $28,000. This loan amount would bring my total loan-to-value ratio, combining the first and second loans, to 80%. This beat out a number of other lenders who would loan up to only 70% or 75%.

Since I was quoted such widely varying terms, my advice to you is to call at least five banks. Even if the first couple of lenders act like you are unreasonable to expect a combined loan-to-value ratio of up to 80% or closing costs which are less than $500, don't give up. I got lucky with my second call (later banks that I called couldn't compete with this bank's good terms), but you may have to search a little harder.

Just remember that the number of small local banks is exploding in this country at the turn of the twenty-first century. There are plenty of banks out there for you to contact, and one of them would really like to have your business, especially if you mention that you reward banks that work with you by giving them additional business. After all, why should you keep your checking and saving accounts with a bank which won't help you as an investor?

# Chapter Eight

# Qualifying Potential Tenants

The beginning landlady or landlord is usually scared of tenants. Even now after years of being a successful landlady, tenant fears will sometimes sneak up on me. They have no basis in my experience. I've had wonderful tenants overall, and even the worst tenants were at the most only annoying.

These fears persist because the faceless tenant is like the unseen bogey man of our childhoods. Our imaginations are fed by the horror stories we're told of protracted eviction battles and of properties maliciously destroyed by vindictive tenants. No one tells us stories about the good tenants. Where is the drama in the tale of people who pay their rent on time and who maintain their rented properties as if they were the owners? These are not interesting stories to tell at parties so we never hear them.

Many tenants are a pleasure to know. If you would like to have tenants like these, you can tilt the odds in your favor. The first step is to choose the right properties. Property selection and tenants are inextricably intertwined. Good properties almost always attract good tenants. I give detailed guidelines on what I consider to be good properties in Chapter Four, Selecting Properties.

Bottom line, the type of tenants you want are people who will insist on renting a nice property. They want it to be clean and in a good neighborhood. Since they are good money managers, they can afford to rent something which is a bit nicer.

The not-so-good tenants will settle for whatever they can get. They may be slovenly or they may have bad credit. They have to rent from people who won't insist on a credit check. They don't have much money so they want inexpensive rental units and non-existent or extremely low security deposits.

If something goes wrong in their financial lives, they have no reserves and few options. Unlike a person renting a property for $1,100 per month who could move into a smaller unit for $550 per month if times got tough, there is no place cheaper for low end tenants to go. Their best option may be to live in your property for free until they get evicted.

## Property Location is Important

Many investment guides focus almost solely on the rate of return a property can generate and ignore the type of tenants any given property will attract. And it is true that a dumpy four-plex located on the corner of two busy streets will produce an amazing cash flow, one far superior to what a nice suburban house will produce.

But you will work hard to earn that higher rate of return. You will spend a lot more of your time handling tenants. After all, who wants to rent a unit in a building with a poor location? Any good tenant who has fallen on hard times will move as soon as she or he can afford to do so. The bad tenants won't have other options. They'll stay until they stop paying the rent at which point you'll have to evict them.

I'm not saying you must buy only single family houses if you want to avoid having tenant problems. Smaller units which are kept in spotless condition will also attract tenants with pride in their home environments if these units are located in a quiet residential area. However, you'll have to sort through a greater quantity of "bad" tenants before you find someone acceptable.

# Eviction Rates

I've taught hundreds of people about rental real estate. During my classes I've surveyed my students to find out how many leases they've signed while they've been in the rental business. Then I've asked them how many tenants they've had to evict. Many of my students have been property owners since the 1970's or 1980's, and have weathered bad times as well as good. The average eviction rate has been 3%.

Out of the nearly forty leases I've had, I've never had to do an eviction, though my sister once posted an eviction notice on one of our joint properties (the tenant paid in full the next day). My father owns seventeen condominiums in a suburb of Denver. Out of almost one hundred leases, he's only had to do four evictions.

A few of my students, though, have experienced eviction rates as high as 50%. When I questioned them, I discovered the following common factors. These students have properties at the low end of the market, the properties are not kept in tip-top condition, and the properties are almost always located in areas of the Denver metro area which are considered extremely undesirable.

You should buy where you would enjoy living. Maybe your personal residence is fairly large because you're older and have several children. But when you look at a condominium as a potential rental unit, it should make you think, "I would have liked to live here when I was young and single". When you look at a starter home, you should think, "This would have been perfect when I was first married". Besides attracting good tenants, desirable properties will give you more liquidity in your real estate investment. If you want or need to sell, you will be able to do it more easily and faster when you have attractive properties.

The second thing you need to do to keep your eviction rate low is to choose good tenants. Even though good tenants won't rent bad properties, the reverse is not true. Bad tenants will still want to rent good properties. Your goal is to eliminate these prospective tenants.

# Finding Tenants

While you may come up with your own creative ways to get tenants, I consider the best sources in descending order to be classified ads, "For Rent" signs, and referrals from tenants or other investors you know.

# Placing Classified Ads

Classified ads are the tried-and-true way to get numerous leads. Unfortunately, running an ad continuously for several weeks straight can add up to a big bill. It's best to keep your ad length short. State the basics such as the number of bedrooms, baths and garage spaces, the rent and deposit amounts, and whether or not pets or smokers are welcome. (In college towns you may want to exclude students as tenants in your ad if the local laws allow you to do this).

Besides the basics, your ad should have a teaser at the very beginning. This is where you mention a special feature of the property. Don't get carried away and list every feature; pick one or two. "Brand New House" is appealing to potential tenants. So is "Luxury Master Suite". List special views of mountains or water. If your rental is located in a popular school district, you could say "Nearly new three bedroom, two bath house in the Eisenhower school district".

Don't put the address of your property in the ad. If you do, it will be difficult to track how many people are interested in your rental. Make them call you to get the address. Even if you leave this information on your voice mail, you'll get the click of a hang-up to tell you that someone called.

If your lease stops at the end of a month, I've found it's best to advertise either five weeks ahead of the vacancy or during the two weeks before the property will be available. Advertising three to four weeks ahead generates far fewer calls and wastes advertising money.

Why does this happen? Because tenants who must give one month's notice look five weeks ahead of the date they hope to move. Tenants who don't pre-plan only look when they are about to move. It may be different in your area, but my advice is not to panic if you get few calls during weeks three and four. I don't even bother to advertise in the newspaper during these weeks.

Lately I've been getting more calls because people saw my ad on the internet. If your newspaper offers to put your classified ad on the web, do it. My local paper, *The Denver Post*, sometimes puts my ads on the web. They don't charge for this service, so I don't complain about the inconsistency, but I have obtained a good tenant who accessed my ad through the internet. I believe this method of advertising will become increasingly important in the future. If you are net savvy, see if your city has a rental site where you can put an ad.

## For Rent Sign

Sticking a sign in the yard is an economical way to generate phone calls, but these people frequently will not want to pay market rent. The property looked nice, so they called. But they were hoping the rent was less. You can, and should, ask for their names and phone numbers in case you drop your asking rent rate later. But usually you will not get a tenant this way.

The major advantage a sign has is as a benefit to your ad callers. When you give the property's address to them so they can drive by, they'll know they have found the correct property when they see your sign.

# Referrals

Getting tenants referred to you is the least expensive way to find them. If one of your tenants gives notice, and they are good tenants, you should ask them if they know someone else who may want to rent the house. You should also tell the rest of your good tenants about this upcoming vacancy. You will, of course, still qualify any suggested tenants, but birds of a feather tend to flock together. Make it clear that you are looking for more good tenants.

Other investors can be your best source of referrals. For example, I ran an ad to rent a house in May, 1998, and ended up with two good applicants. A friend of mine had a vacancy coming up in the middle of June. Fortunately, one of the tenants had to give thirty days notice, and they decided to take the other property. That was the easiest vacancy to fill that my friend ever had.

# Who Are Your Prospective Tenants?

Tenants come from a broad spectrum of people. The most obvious group are students. Any area near a college campus will have a huge tenant market. However, students are not my idea of ideal tenants. They are young and careless. They don't know how to maintain properties, and they are liable to leave before their leases are up.

If you live in a college town, you may or may not be allowed to discriminate against students. They are not protected by any federal laws, but your state or city may have passed local laws prohibiting discrimination against students. In this situation, if you don't want to rent to students, you should buy properties as far away from campus as possible. Avoid properties next to bus routes as well. This will make your properties less desirable to the type of tenants you want to avoid. You'll still sometimes have students as tenants, but not as often.

Even though I live close to Boulder, a city with a large student population, I purchase rental houses in the suburbs of Denver instead. The higher rents students pay are not high enough for me to endure the additional property damage and management duties. My target tenants are responsible adults who for some reason prefer not to own their own homes.

It may be hard for you to imagine someone who wants to rent instead of own. You are the type of person who understands the benefits of being a property owner or you wouldn't be reading this book. You understand that real estate is the best way for most people to acquire wealth. For most families their home is their most valuable asset. Why would intelligent, responsible people choose to rent?

I've encountered a number of valid reasons. Sometimes tenants are in the process of a divorce. Until it is final they will not be able to qualify for a loan. Since divorcing spouses rarely continue to share their old home, one of them must rent a place. A divorcing parent will want a house for the kids instead of an apartment if he or she can afford it.

Young adults who are not sure where they want to settle down will prefer to rent for a while. I've rented to groups of singles and to newly married couples. These tenants will eventually buy their own homes, but they may rent from you for a couple of years before they move on.

Some tenants have owned houses in areas which recently experienced a market downturn. Several of my Colorado tenants came from California. California real estate did not do well in the mid-nineties. These people are real estate shy. Like the cat who won't jump on either a hot or cold stove after being burned once, these tenants are reluctant to buy a house even in an appreciating market.

Some tenants are new to an area. Before they buy a house, they want a chance to investigate the various neighborhoods. Although these tenants tend to move as soon as their lease runs out, they are excellent tenants in the meantime.

Other tenants are corporate employees who know they will be transferred again. Rather than go through the hassle of buying and selling a house, they decide it's easier to rent. They know they will never stay in one place long enough to benefit from appreciation, not after they subtract closing costs. They plan to make their money through a great job, not through owning real estate.

All of these people can be great tenants. They are out there looking for a wonderful place to live. If you take the trouble to buy and maintain special rental properties, you will be able to select from the best tenants available. You'll be able to take pride in providing a valuable service to the community while furthering your financial goals.

# Screening Phone Calls

Depending on how hot your local rental market is, you may get a deluge of calls or just a slow trickle. The Denver area was experiencing a fairly tight rental market in the summer of 1998. When I placed an ad for a property at the end of June, I received between two and three calls per day. In the winter I receive that many calls per week.

You should have a list of questions you want to ask when a potential tenant calls. You should also include on your list additional information you want to tell callers, information you didn't include in the ad itself. If you know that your property has a drawback such as no basement, mention it up front. Ask the tenant if that will be a problem for them. It's better to find this out immediately rather than after you've talked to someone for five minutes.

If you allow pets on a negotiable basis, find out what pets they have. Most pet owners will volunteer this information immediately. If you won't accept their pet, the phone call is probably over.

You should ask when the tenants need to move because it won't always be the same date as when your rental will be going vacant. If someone calls me about a property available the first of this month, but they want it for the first of next month, I volunteer to split the month with them. I remind them that the extra two weeks will give them plenty of time to move. Almost everyone will agree to this compromise if they like your property.

Make sure to tell the caller about any amenities you didn't mention in the ad. Tell them if your property is located only two blocks away from the elementary school or the city recreation center. Tell them about the public swimming pools, parks, and bicycle trails.

## Short-Term and Long-Term Tenants

You also want to know how long a tenant plans to rent. Be careful about accepting short-term leases. You will soon be facing the hassle of renting your property again, plus you'll have the additional damage caused by more people moving in and out of the house. Short-term tenants, however, will rarely be willing to pay you a significant rent premium in order to compensate you for these problems.

Tell people interested in short-term leases that you might consider taking them if you don't find a long-term tenant during the next two weeks. Volunteer to take their names and phone numbers so you can call them back if the property is still available. Maybe you will be happy to take a short-term tenant at that time, but you should give yourself a chance to find a long-term tenant instead.

One benefit many tenants want is a property owner who has deliberately chosen that role. One third of the tenants who call on my ads are being forced to move because the house they are currently renting is being sold. If you let them know you are a professional property owner, someone who intends to hold onto your rental properties for years, you will be reassuring them that they will not be forced to move again. Indeed, you would be thrilled to have a long-term tenant.

## Showing Your Properties

When you start to receive calls on your properties, don't rush right out to show them each time someone calls. You can waste a lot of time this way. Prospective tenants will drive by a property, decide they don't like the exterior, then not bother to show up for their appointments.

You can avoid this problem by advising them to drive by the property first, then call you back if they are interested in seeing the interior. Be sure to remind them not to peer in the windows or wander into the backyard if someone still lives there.

Whenever you agree to show a property, try to cluster a group of showings close together. If a prospective tenant wants to see the property at two in the afternoon, tell the next caller you could show it to them at one forty-five or two-fifteen. Since some of your prospective tenants won't show up for their appointments, you'll increase your chances of a productive trip by scheduling more than one showing.

The ultimate in scheduling all prospective tenants at the same time is to hold a rental open house. Advertise your property in the rental section as usual, but include open house hours. Make sure the newspaper doesn't stick your ad in houses for sale like they did to me once. Hold the open house on a Saturday. Many tenants set aside one weekend to find a rental house. If they can find something they like on Saturday, they won't wait to see other houses on Sunday.

# Avoiding Dangerous People

You should realize that not all prospective tenants are looking for a house to rent. They may not be tenants at all. While rare, you may find yourself showing an empty house to someone who is dangerous. When I schedule a showing, I get that person's name and phone number and tell them I'll have to check if I can show the property at the time we've agreed on. Then I call them back. At least I now have a phone number where they can be reached. Then I give this information to my husband or business partner.

When you show the property, it's best if you have someone with you. I tell my current tenants to feel free to stay in the house during showings. Sometimes I take my husband or sister with me when I show the property. If I'm doing a rental open house, I always have someone with me.

Sometimes you will decide to show properties alone. Tell the tenant that you told other people you would be at the property showing it, and that you invited them to drop by at the same time. I leave this invitation on my answering machine in case other potential tenants call so somebody else could indeed be showing up unexpectedly.

I don't want to scare you unduly with this advice, but you should be careful. Each year a few real estate agents, both male and female, are killed showing properties to buyers they don't know. Property owners face many of the same risks as agents. Though it's unlikely you'll encounter someone dangerous, it's best to be cautious.

# Bad and Good Tenants

Who is a bad tenant? Your definition must comply with all federal, state, and local laws. If your definition of an undesirable tenant includes someone with children, I sympathize. Children do tend to cause damage. However, it's illegal to select your tenants based on family status. I'll tell you more about these protected classes later in this chapter in the Fair Housing Section.

You do have the right to discriminate based on other criteria which are perfectly legal. I use a number of criteria to qualify prospective tenants as either desirable or undesirable. First, will they make the monthly rent payments? This involves more than having an adequate income to pay the rent. I once had some female tenants who danced at a strip club. They made a lot of money, but paying their rent wasn't always their number one priority.

You may decide not to rent to people with certain professions. This is usually legal if you are consistent. Some local governments, though, may prohibit restrictions against certain types of employment. For example, the city of Denver prohibits discrimination against people employed in the military.

Another group of tenants I've learned to avoid based on other property owners' experiences are those people who rely on someone else to help them pay the rent. These people range from trust fund babies to people receiving financial help from their parents to Section 8 recipients.

Regarding Section 8, I will say I've met landlords who love this government sponsored program. The government pays part of the rent payments, and it's easy to find new Section 8 tenants. You may be willing to participate in this program, but realize that you could be required to allow Section 8 tenants in all of your properties if you decide to accept a Section 8 tenant in even one of your properties. Since leases will not end all at the same time because of the occasional broken lease (the tenant leaves early), you may not be able to exit the program once you start.

You will also have Big Brother supervising you. If you and Big Brother disagree, Big Brother has an unlimited source of bureaucrats to harass you. And just to drive you crazy, not every bureaucrat will interpret the rules the same way. It's the nature of working with the government. Personally, I'm not interested in this program, but it may suit you just fine. Try to talk to other investors in your area to find out what their experiences have been with the local bureaucrats.

I want tenants who have to earn their rent payments by working. These tenants, in my opinion, are more responsible and desirable. They know how hard they must work to make those monthly payments, and they appreciate the money and time I've invested in their rental homes.

## Adequate Incomes

How do you decide if a tenant's income will be sufficient to cover the rent yet leave enough for the tenant to pay other expenses? I like the rent amount to equal less than thirty percent of the tenants' monthly income, but I can be flexible if they have little other monthly debt that must be paid. I may let the rent go as high as forty percent of their income if they don't have car or student loan payments.

Sometimes people are self-employed. This makes it almost impossible to verify their incomes. Even if you get them to show you their last tax return, you will know that they did their best to minimize the income they reported. So what do you do? The best way to see if someone will pay their rent, and pay it on time, is to look at their credit record. Anyone who wants to rent from me must fill out a rental application.

Many companies exist who will provide credit checking services for property owners (they will also usually provide you with a rental application to use). Look in the phone book under "Credit Reports". The credit reporting company will have forms for you to complete in order to be allowed to use their services. Do this well in advance of advertising for tenants. When you get a rental application, you want to be able to get the credit check run quickly.

The credit reporting company I use lets me fax in the rental application in the morning and calls me back with the results late that afternoon. If prospective tenants have a great financial track record, I will probably accept them, even when I can't verify their incomes.

I do, however, look out for tenants with high credit card balances, car payments, and student loans. They may have managed to juggle all their bills until now, but I don't want everything to go delinquent while they are living in my property. Someone who declares bankruptcy can prolong an eviction, and in the meantime I may not be getting any rent.

Sometimes I will take a tenant with a bad credit history. These are the people who will most likely stay the longest in a property because they can't qualify to buy a house. If the blotch on the credit history comes with a good story, such as a past lapse of health insurance combined with a health problem, I'll try to verify the story. In one case the prospective tenants said the wife's Cesaeran delivery had not been covered by health insurance. Their credit report showed a write-off from a doctor and a hospital two years ago, and they had a two-year-old child. Since their other bills were current, I decided to accept these applicants.

While I may make an exception for this type of credit problem, I never make exceptions when a past landlord or landlady has reported late rent payments or an actual eviction surfaces. My sister once had an applicant who had been evicted twice in the previous thirteen months! The tenant claimed it was an error on the part of the credit bureau. Shelley expressed sympathy and invited the tenant to re-apply after the tenant's credit report had been corrected. Until then, the tenant's application was declined.

If you do decide to reject a potential tenant based on a bad credit report, then the Fair Credit Reporting Act requires you to do the following. You must give the applicant the name of the credit reporting agency, explain that the credit agency didn't make the decision to reject them (you did), and let them know they have the right to get a copy of their credit report. They may then dispute the report and present their side of the story by adding a consumer statement to the report.

If you have any questions about what you must do in this situation, ask the company who ran the credit report for you to give you guidance. Remember that these requirements are designed to alert consumers to their credit reporting rights. They do not mean that you must accept people with bad credit as tenants.

## Maintaining a Property

When you're evaluating whether or not tenants will maintain a property in good condition, you can ask about their home maintenance skills. You can look at the way they dress, the way their car looks, and how their children behave. If the kids are sliding down the banisters while you are showing the house, and the parents don't seem to notice or care, this is going to be a problem.

I love renting to previous homeowners. They come complete with a toolbox, hose, lawn mower, and plenty of experience fixing the little things. By the way, I don't provide snow shovels, hoses, and lawn mowers to my tenants who rent houses. I tell them they will have to buy these items as part of the privilege of living in a single family house. This saves me a bit of money, but more importantly I'm not responsible for maintaining and replacing these items. Nor am I as liable if someone hurts themselves using equipment they, not I, own.

## Long-Term Tenants

A long-term tenant is much better than a short-term tenant, but it's not always easy to predict how long someone will rent from you. Even young couples who you would think would want to buy their own home may take years to do it. Other couples happily break their leases early and sacrifice part of their deposit if they locate a house they want to buy.

I have found no consistent pattern except for two exceptions. If people say they are under contract to buy a new house which will be done in four to eight months, they will be moving soon. People with a questionable credit history, however, will usually renew their leases because they need time to repair their financial reputation.

My advice is to avoid the obvious short-term tenants who are buying houses. Only take them if you are getting desperate for someone with good credit. These people generally are great credit risks. They need to qualify for a loan to buy their new house so they will pay the rent on time. However, you will soon be looking for replacement tenants.

The people with questionable credit are a calculated risk. They already have bad credit so they don't have as much to lose by incurring another ding from you, but they could turn out to be wonderful long-term tenants. A long-term tenant translates into less time, money and energy managing your properties, so they are a valuable commodity. If they have shown a consistent pattern of placing their rent at the top of their financial priority list, these tenants can be wonderful.

## Accepting Pets

I allow pets on a negotiable basis since it gives me a much broader pool of tenants. So far none of my tenants' pets have done substantial damage to any of my properties. I believe my good fortune has been due to selecting good tenants. Responsible people who pay their bills and take pride in their personal living enviroment do not allow their pets to destroy a house.

I want to know the ages of any pets. Puppies make puddles, and old dogs become incontinent. Unfixed animals, whether feline or canine, get into trouble. Even an unfixed female cat may spray in the house. I want animals who are middle aged for their breed and who don't have the ability to reproduce.

I also watch out for tenants who talk about their pets as beloved members of the family. I have cats, and I adore them, but I know they are pets. Some people are inordinately attached to their animals, and will forgive them any wrong, including destroying my properties. I don't want to rent to people who coo when they talk about Fido or Fluffy.

## The Trouble with Smokers

I'm much tougher when it comes to smokers. Smoke makes its way into the carpets and the drapes. It discolors the walls and ceilings. Once a property has been rented to a smoker, especially a heavy smoker, non-smokers may not be willing to rent it until the drapes and carpets have been cleaned and the walls repainted.

If a smoker tells me he or she only smokes outside, I don't believe them. The weather gets cold. It gets hot. Sometimes it rains or snows. Why will these people worry about my no-smoking rules when it's unpleasant outside? Every smoker I know gets tempted to break this agreement, even when married to a disapproving spouse who will find out as soon as she or he comes home and smells the tell-tale smoke.

Fortunately, few people smoke in my tenant price range. As a real estate broker, I noticed that the less expensive a house was, the more likely it was for the owner to smoke. If I owned smaller units, I would probably have to allow some smokers. As it is, my ads state pets negotiable, no smokers. I'd rather deal with a bare spot in the lawn than the persistent odor of smoke.

## Argumentative Tenants

You will talk to some strange people when you advertise a property for rent. One gentleman who called told me he had an unfixed dog. Whoops. I told him the animal would have to be neutered. Okay, said the prospective tenant. He'd do it after he moved here.

I told him it would have to be done within thirty days, not totally happy with the idea of letting him move in with an unfixed dog. Did I really want to risk fighting with him if he later changed his mind? Plus, it was a bulldog. The owner said it was as gentle as could be, but bulldogs were named that because of their ability to take down bulls. My alarm bells were starting to ring.

Then the prospective gentleman told me he was moving to Colorado because he was going to start his own business. "Wonderful," I thought, "the guy doesn't have a stable source of income." And then he added that he needed three bedrooms so his live-in girlfriend's parents could visit. Why? Because they helped her out financially and in return they expected a bedroom so they could visit.

You can guess how thrilled I was at this point. Rather than bluntly turn the guy down, I explained that if I did decide to rent the property to him, I would need the security deposit up front, in good-as-cash funds. This would be necessary if he wanted me to hold the house for him until he took possession in two weeks.

This guy was already reminding me of a smarmy salesman with his I'm-your-pal attitude, and now he complained that I was nicking him too much. Why couldn't I just take an out-of-state check? He wouldn't be home for a week, and therefore couldn't go to his bank for a cashier's check until then.

I wrapped up our conversation fairly quickly. This prospective tenant didn't understand that it was my valuable property we were discussing, and therefore I made the rules. All my requirements are legal and consistent, and I wasn't going to be badgered into changing them for his benefit. I told him that perhaps he could find some other property owner who was more flexible and reasonable than I was. I was relieved to say a firm good-bye and hang up.

As soon as you find yourself with someone who wants to argue about your rules, you know you have a problem tenant. Most people will respect your positions when you explain them. Look at this situation; why would I want to risk keeping a property vacant for two weeks at a cost of $620 in lost rent while I waited for an out-of-state check to clear?

Most people understand that you need your deposit in good-as-cash funds. If they are flying home the next day, they can overnight you a cashier's check. Or they can get a cash advance on their credit cards from a local bank. Reasonable people understand that you need your deposit as soon as possible, or else you'll have to rent to someone else.

There is a certain type of person who slides through life by haranguing other people into bending the rules. Then these people take advantage of this kindness by trying to bend the rules even further. Shelley's prospective tenant with the two recent evictions called frequently over a two week period trying to wear my sister down into taking her as a tenant despite her crummy credit.

While this type of prospective tenant is rare, you should know how to recognize one and be ready to tell them you will not rent to them. If they are hard to handle during the interview process, imagine what it will be like arguing for your rent every month. This type of tenant produces great stories, but in the meantime he or she will make you regret ever buying a rental property. Remember that what you want is just as important as what some tenant wants, and since you have the power to choose, say good-bye to unpleasant people.

# Perfect and Good Enough Tenants

Some property owners I know spend weeks looking for the perfect tenants. My time is too valuable for that. I look for the good enough tenants. The first person who meets my requirements gets the property. If a second person wants to apply at the same time, I sometimes run credit checks on both prospective tenants, but if I've charged them both a credit checking fee, I reimburse the credit fee to the tenant I turn down.

If you like the idea of having numerous applicants to choose among, you should set your rents a bit below the market rate. The more aggressively you discount your rents, the more applicants you will have, and the choosier you can be.

The market for rentals is constantly changing. If the market in your area gets soft, I do recommend lowering your rent rather than dropping your standards for an acceptable tenant. A reduced rental amount is worth it in exchange for high quality tenants. But remember that a good enough tenant doesn't mean the first person who says "I'll take it" when they see your property.

When I advertised one house for rent, I had six sets of people look at it over the weekend. My current tenant showed the property since I was out of town (though I was regularly checking my messages and calling back the people who wanted to schedule a showing).

One set of tenants announced on Saturday that they would take the property. The husband smelled of smoke (though he said he was a non-smoker), and the family had a fifteen-week-old Rottweiler puppy. On Sunday a young man with a temporary job announced that he and his roommate wanted to rent the house. He was glad the landlady had a no smoking policy; he wanted her to make sure his roommate kept his agreement to only smoke outside.

Three other tenants said the house wouldn't work for them, and the last set was non-committal. This family had particularly impressed my tenant. The children were well-behaved, the parents did not smell like smokers, and overall they seemed like pleasant people.

Even though I felt the pressure to accept one of the applications from the two sets of prospective tenants who said they wanted the property, I told them no. Both were probably going to smoke in the house, and then I'd have the hassle of evicting them before they turned the house yellow and stinky.

Since the one man had stated he didn't smoke, I didn't address that issue. Why argue about whether or not he really did smoke? I told his wife that a puppy didn't go well with the new flower garden I was putting into the backyard (fifteen feet by fifty-five feet). This reason was true as well, and had the advantage of being irrefutable.

I was prepared to run my ad again, but luckily the non-committal tenants called back. They had decided they wanted the property. Their credit wasn't perfect, but it came with a good story. They wanted to rent for two to three years while they got their finances in order, and then buy a house. Because the father was allergic, they would never be getting a cat or dog.

I accepted these tenants. They weren't perfect because of the marred credit, but they were good enough. The other two sets of tenants were not. Sometimes it can be difficult to draw the line, true, but you must be comfortable with the tenants in your properties. It's like a marriage - both of you should be excited and pleased. Making someone unhappy by telling them no is unpleasant, but your reward will be getting a better tenant eventually.

# Fair Housing Laws

Federal, state and local laws exist which place restrictions on how property owners select tenants. These laws are designed to eliminate discrimination against certain classes of people.

State and local laws go beyond the federal laws by adding protected classes and providing for other tenant protections and benefits. For example, the city of Boulder prohibits discrimination based on sexual orientation, thereby adding a protected class, and the city also requires 5% interest to be paid on security deposits, which is a benefit for tenants.

The federal Fair Housing Act prohibits discrimination on the basis of race, color, religion, sex, national origin, disability and familial status. All residential property must comply with a limited number of exceptions.

For example, if you own a four-plex and live in one of the units, the other units are not covered by the federal law. Also, if a single family home is offered for sale or rent **by the owner**, discrimination is allowed 1) if the owner does not use the services of a rental or real estate agent or anyone in the business of selling real estate; 2) the owner does not own or have an interest in more than three single family homes; and 3) the owner does not engage in any illegal advertising.

These amazing exceptions, I believe, were allowed under the assumption that small time property owners could not be expected to comply with the Fair Housing Act due to lack of education and awareness. Many states such as Colorado have enacted laws which eliminate these exceptions (Colorado only allows familial status to be used as a basis of discrimination in the previously described small property owner situations). In addition, Colorado law applies to all property, including commercial property, whereas the federal law applies only to residential property.

There are two key things you can do to stay on the right side of the law. First, obtain something in writing from your state department of housing which details your state's fair housing laws, and also check with the housing departments of the cities where you own or plan to own rental property.

Second, be consistent in how you treat potential tenants. When people call on ads, ask everyone the same questions and give everyone the same additional information (this is where your written lists come in handy). Be careful not to inadvertently get into trouble.

An example of accidentally making yourself liable to accusations of discrimination could occur in the following way. Some tenants in a protected class (which includes everyone) call about your property. Let's say they have a dog and you tell them you don't take pets.

Three weeks later the property is still vacant, and you decide to accept pets after all. You rent to someone with a dog. This person is not in the same protected class as the first set of tenants who liked your property. They see the dog, and accuse you of refusing to rent to them because of who they are.

How do you protect yourself in a situation like this? By asking for everyone's name and number when you turn them down due to some requirement that could change. They smoke? Tell them you currently hope to get a tenant who does not, but you would like to take their name and number in case you change your mind. Ditto for income requirements, pet ownership, house maintenance skills, anything that you hope to get in a tenant but may not insist upon.

You can also protect yourself by keeping records of your previous tenants. Supposedly you are blind when it comes to the protected classes, but wouldn't it be nice to produce a list of past tenants who lived in your properties with children if you ever get accused of discriminating based on familial status? You get the idea. Don't throw out those old leases; keep them in a file somewhere.

If you ever have any questions about fair housing laws and how they might apply in a particular circumstance, call your state's department of fair housing. It may be called something different so you may have to do some sleuthing. Other common names are the Civil Rights Commission, the Open Housing Commission, or the Department/Commission of Human Affairs or Human Rights. The staff should be able to answer your questions and provide information on your state laws.

# Chapter Nine

## Day to Day Details

This chapter is a collection of tidbits which can make your life as a property owner run more smoothly.

## Property Insurance

Getting good insurance policies on your rental properties will protect you against losing your investments. Since insurance is regulated by the states, the insurance available where you live may not include some of the coverage I'm about to suggest. The two states where I own properties, Texas and Colorado, handle property insurance very differently.

Policies with different levels of coverage are offered for rental properties. Check with your insurance agent for information on the types of policies available in your state. I believe it is worth the small extra cost to get a more comprehensive policy rather than the most basic policy you must get to satisfy your lender.

Why? Because most property owners aren't scared by the thought of potential damage caused by a storm or flood. Instead, they have nightmares about malicious tenants who punch holes in the walls and reach in to cut the electrical wires. They've heard the stories about tenants who lock their dogs in the house for weeks at a time without ever letting them out to relieve themselves. Or the tenants who build fires in the bathtub and tenants who stain all the carpets.

Fixing this type of damage is bad enough; not being insured for it and having to pay for the repairs out-of-pocket is worse. It's possible to get an All Risk landlord policy where excessive property damage will be classified as vandalism by the insurance company. Not only will the insurance company pay for the cost of restoring the property back to its previous condition, but in addition the property owner will be covered for the cost of lost rent while the property is being repaired.

This is the type of coverage I have on my Colorado properties. If you are the vindictive sort, rest assured that the insurance company will go after your ex-tenants to try to collect reimbursement for its claim expenses. This saves you the time, expense, and effort of chasing them down yourself to get satisfaction for a judgement against them. Do be careful how you handle the security deposit, however. My guess is you can't subtract funds for anything that was covered by your insurance. Always check with an attorney if you find yourself in a complicated situation.

This warning about keeping too much of the security deposit won't apply in most cases. Malicious tenants are usually evicted for failure to pay their rent. Whatever security deposit you have will probably be swallowed up whole by the tenant's unpaid rent; just make sure your lease allows you to apply the deposit toward rent. And remember, while the insurance company pays for lost rent due to the time needed to repair vandalism, I've never heard of a policy that reimburses property owners for any of the costs involved in an eviction.

## Renter's Insurance

Some property owners require their tenants to get renter's insurance and to provide proof that they have done this. If you require a certificate of insurance, you can have it set up so you'll be notified if the tenant cancels the coverage. My insurance agent thinks that making a rental insurance policy a requirement is a good idea, but I only recommend it to my tenants. I have so many other requirements that I hesitate to add one more.

I do explain at the time the lease is signed that renter's insurance is a relatively inexpensive policy that protects the personal belongings of the tenant. For example, if my tenant's Christmas tree catches fire in the family room, and most of the tenant's furniture in that room is destroyed, the damage to the house will be covered under the landlord's insurance policy. The damage to the furniture will not be covered. This is because the owner's landlord policy only covers the house, not any of the contents.

For a cost of under $200 per year in most areas of the United States, tenants can purchase a renter's insurance policy that will provide coverage for their personal possessions. Some insurance companies such as Farmer's Insurance will automatically include a $100,000 liability policy as part of the renter's insurance.

This liabilty policy protects the tenant in case they accidentally damage your property. Instead of losing their security deposit, they can file a claim and only have to pay their deductible. Going back to the example of the Christmas tree fire, your insurance company could decide that your tenants' negligence was responsible for the fire and the resulting damage. In that case the tenants' liability policy will hopefully cover them. Otherwise, they may be facing a very large bill presented by your insurance company.

Most renter's insurance policies will also provide for additional living expenses. For example, if that Christmas tree fire damages the house badly enough to force the tenants to move out, most renter's policies will provide money to pay for a short-term rental while the house is being repaired.

If you explain to your tenants how much protection they can get for a small annual payment, they will probably want renter's insurance. Even if they have few valuable possessions, they may be reassured to know that if they accidentally damage your property, they'll only have to pay a deductible. Make it very clear that they must rely on the insurance agent's explanation of the coverage they are buying instead of your inexpert explanation.

## Best Rental Months

Hopefully, your old lease will end during one of the hot rental months. June and July are the best months, but May and August are close runner-ups. Next best are April and September. The worst month of all is December. Almost no one chooses to move at this time of year. Calls from prospective tenants will be few and far between.

When you sign a lease, try to get the last month to land in the summer. I've done leases shorter or longer than a year in order to do this. However, if you are still at the point of acquiring properties, realize that some lenders will want to see leases of one year or longer on all of your properties. A shorter lease may cause you problems when you apply for your next loan.

Whether short or long leases are better is a matter of opinion. On one hand many tenants will honor a longer lease. At the least, if they break it early, you can use their security deposit to cover the lost rent until you re-rent the property. In return, though, you are also stuck in a long lease. If your tenants are doing something you hate, you may not be able to get rid of them until the end of the lease.

For example, say your tenant never waters the lawn. Week after week it's you who is out there moving the hose. The lease says the tenant is responsible, but an eviction judge might not consider this breach of the lease to be important enough to justify an eviction. A tenant's right to keep his or her home is very powerful. In other words, if you try to evict the tenant for not watering the lawn, the judge may not rule in your favor.

Or you may have a tenant who pays the rent late every month. In Colorado, even if you have to start an eviction proceeding each and every month in order to get your tenant to pay the rent, as long as the tenant pays by the third business day after you post the eviction notice, you're stuck accepting the rent plus any late fee. It may drive you crazy and it may be a waste of your time, but you'll have to do this every month they are late with the rent until the lease ends. Make sure your late fee is big enough to compensate you for your time.

Your only consolation will be to report your tenants to the credit bureaus for paying their rent late. But I wouldn't do this until after they've moved out. It's not good to make a tenant angry who still has possession of one of your properties.

My leases have ranged from six months to fifteen months. Overall, I've decided that I prefer to sign longer leases when possible. If tenants are difficult, I do have the time to water lawns and post eviction notices. Fortunately, so far I have had only occasional problems which were resolved with one or two phone calls. Long-term leases have been good for my rental business.

# Emergency Fund

Every property owner should have an emergency fund savings account. This money will allow you to sleep easily because if a furnace needs to be replaced, a tenant evicted, or a long vacancy endured, you will have cash in hand to cover these costs.

Your emergency fund should be kept in an account which is separate from your personal savings. Its sole purpose is to be used as short-term operating funds for your real estate investment business. Resist the urge to borrow from it to pay for personal expenses, or the money won't be there when you need it.

My personal emergency fund consisted of $2,000 for each property until I reached $5,000 in my savings account. At that point I stopped adding any additional money because the majority of my properties produce cash flow. Whenever I have to dip into my emergency account, I replenish it as soon as possible. Since I have a number of properties generating extra money each month, it doesn't take long to get my balance back to $5,000.

You may want to keep more or less money in your emergency fund depending on your financial circumstances and the price range of your properties. If you are investing in an expensive part of the country and have mortgage payments which average $2,000 compared to my average minimum required payment of $850, you may want to adjust your emergency fund balance upwards. Conversely, if you are investing in an inexpensive area, $5,000 in your emergency fund may be excessive.

# How to Have Happy Tenants

You'll make your tenants happy by doing two things: respecting them as the people who are helping you to achieve your financial goals, and by keeping your properties in good to excellent condition. Always call your tenants before you come by a property to make repairs or to show it to new prospective tenants. It is their home. You should get your tenants' permission whenever you want to enter their home, especially if they won't be there when you come by the house.

Whenever you have contact with your tenants, you should ask them if they are having any problems with their houses. Some things that bother them may not be solvable. You can't do much about the yappy neighbor's dog who barks at them whenever they sit outside. But at least you can be sympathetic while you explain that there isn't much you can do.

I tend to give tenants a small gift when they re-sign a new one year lease. A pretty gift basket with a note thanking them for being such great tenants is a good way to communicate how glad you are to have them in your property. After all, these people are paying off your mortgage for you (and I assume you wouldn't have renewed the lease unless they've been good tenants).

In the spring, I try to come by each property at least once to do a spring weeding and to trim the bushes and trees. Many tenants help or provide refreshments. They generally appreciate the improvement in their yards and do their best to maintain them the rest of the year.

This also gives me a chance to visit with my tenants. Once they know me as a person they are more likely to treat me well. It's much easier for people to cause problems for a stranger rather than for someone they know. You'll be rewarded if you get to know your tenants on a casual basis. Your tenants will treat you and your property with more respect.

## Maintaining Your Properties

Your goal should be to keep your properties in salable condition at all times since you never know when you may decide to sell them. Deferred maintenance can be overwhelming when it must be handled all at once. Because a house is so large, something always needs a little attention. This makes perfection an unreachable goal, but it is worthwhile as a target.

Tenants will usually perceive your efforts as a benefit to them. Even when you are making improvements such as landscaping the backyard in order to raise the value of the property, they will feel that you are doing the work for their increased enjoyment. Many times tenants will even volunteer to help you. They are happy to live in a nicer environment, and your property is maintaining or increasing in value. It's a win-win situation.

You should keep a careful eye on your houses. Touch up the paint on the south and west sides. Watch the trim and keep it painted. These areas are the first ones to lose their paint coverage, so if you spend a little extra time painting them yourself, you can postpone hiring a painter to repaint the entire house. Never let your paint job get so old that it fails to protect your siding. Installing new siding is expensive!

When you bought your properties, you should have hired a professional to inspect them. Maintaining your properties means having an inspector come back every two to three years to inspect the properties again. A good inspector will charge a reasonable fee (I pay $100). He or she will alert you to incipient problems. You'll know when sinks are about to rust out, a hot water heater is set to go, or a damp crawl space is indicating drainage problems.

You can take care of these problems before they become emergencies. This means you can handle these items at your convenience. Periods of vacancy are perfect for doing any interior maintenance. Even if you have very long-term tenants you should still have the properties inspected, then schedule the maintenance work to be done when it's least inconvenient to your tenants.

Work may be as minor as re-caulking the bathtub tile or something as major as replacing the furnace because the heat exchanger cracked. You may also want to provide new furnace filters each fall as a reminder that you expect the tenants to change them on a monthly basis.

## Major Repairs and Maintenance

I usually wait for vacancies to do major interior work unless the tenants are very long-term. But long-term tenants rarely ask for much maintenance work. So I wait until they move out before I touch up the paint, replace any carpeting or vinyl flooring, or install new counter tops.

Whenever I do any of these projects, I don't do them piecemeal. New carpet in the living areas usually means new carpet in the bedrooms as well. Most investment books will say it's okay to have different colors of carpet in different rooms, but that's not what you'll see in new homes. Buyers of houses do not like a hodge podge of carpet, and neither do desirable tenants.

When it comes to choosing a carpet color, do not automatically choose a boring beige. Vacant houses with beige carpet, white walls, and off-white blinds are depressingly bland whether you're trying to sell them or rent them. It's okay to add color in the carpet, a wallpaper border, or in the drapes. Window valances are inexpensive and can be removed if a tenant doesn't like them.

A cut berber carpet is my favorite. It looks luxurious and the mixture of three to four different colors hides everyday wear and tear quite well. If you want a more standard plush carpet, always get trackless and look at colors such as a grayed blue or muted rose. If you must get a beige, get a warm one with tones of pink instead of yellow. Taupe is far superior to a boring tan.

I aim for a moderate price range on my carpets, neither the cheapest nor the most expensive. I want something nice enough to attract tenants who want a lovely home, but not so expensive that if it's damaged it will be financially very painful. I plan and budget for replacing carpet every twelve to fourteen years. If I'm lucky, it will last longer, but I don't count on it.

## Refrigerators, Washers and Dryers

Many tenants have their own appliances. If they don't, I tell them about used appliance stores in the area. Most used appliance stores charge around $400 for either a refrigerator or a washer and dryer. The items are usually warranted for a year, which is the length of my typical lease. I also tell my tenants about companies which will rent appliances for a monthly fee. If you want to be prepared with prices or rental rates, call companies in the phone book and ask for information before you show a property. Look under "Appliances - Used" or "Appliances - Rental".

Because most of my tenants have supplied their own appliances, I don't get phone calls telling me the refrigerator isn't keeping food cold enough, or that the washing machine is making a funny sound. These are the tenants' problems, and I never find out about them. They don't cost me money and, most importantly, they don't create hassle in my life.

If you've purchased a property which came with appliances, you can exclude these items on the lease. State clearly that they are not included as part of the property, but that you will leave them as a convenience for your tenants. If your tenants should ever decide they don't want them, they should notify you and you will have them removed. Make it very clear that any appliance maintenance is not your responsibility. If tenants want a broken appliance repaired, they may do so at their own expense.

My properties do come with dishwashers and stoves since these items are rarely owned by tenants. If a heating element goes out, most tenants are willing to buy a new element and install it themselves. I tell them to send me the bill so I can reimburse them. I never let tenants deduct expenses from their rent due. Doing that messes up my records, and doing taxes is a big enough bother as it is.

## Vacancies

Your vacancy rate will go through cycles. Why? Because you may go through two or three tenants before you find a tenant who sticks. This person, for whatever reason, does not move on. Instead of having to look for a new tenant each year, you will instead give modest rent raises to your current tenant. Besides a bit of routine maintenance, you'll hardly spend any time managing this property.

Even long-term tenants will eventually move on and you'll have to start the renting process over again. You'll go through another quick succession of tenants before you find the next long-term tenant. In the worst case scenario all of your long-term tenants will move in the same year, creating a glut of work in a short period of time, but other years no one will move.

Talk to your tenants on a regular basis so you know when to expect vacancies. Make room in your schedule to handle repairs and for showing the property. Once you've owned your properties for awhile, you may discover that you have to re-lease fewer than half of them each year.

If your average tenant is staying for two years, you can allow up to one month of vacancy each time a tenant moves out and still only average one half month of vacancy per property per year. You'll have plenty of time to make repairs and interview new tenants.

Frequently I experience no down time between tenants. My lease allows me to show a property more than six weeks before the lease ends. As long as my current tenants keep a decently clean house that shows well, new tenants will sign a lease before the old tenants move out.

Other times I purposely create a vacancy. If I know that I plan to repaint and replace the carpeting and vinyl flooring, then I don't bother to advertise the property until I've made the improvements. Of course, I also raise the rent substantially. Tenants will pay a premium for brand new carpeting and paint.

## Hiring a Property Manager

Always manage your own properties if possible. Why? First, because you'll qualify as an active investor who can take advantage of the tax savings due to the depreciation of your properties. If you do hire a property manager, you should make sure you still meet the requirements of being an active investor. You should help set rent rates and approve tenants in order to qualify by the Internal Revenue Service guidelines. This is an area where you should certainly check with your accountant for specific advice on the precise definition of an active investor.

But the biggest reason not to hire a property manager is the cost. Let's say you rent your property for $1,000 a month and after paying your mortgage payment which includes taxes and insurance, your cash flow is $250 per month. You still have to pay for average maintenance costs of at least $100 per month. The property manager may charge you 10% of the monthly rent, or $100. This leaves you with a cash flow of $50 a month, or $600 per year. If you have two weeks of vacancy per year at a cost of $500, you'll net only $100 a year in cash flow. Putting less than $10 a month into your pocket when it could be eleven times that amount for a small amount of work seems silly to me.

## You Can Manage Your Own Properties

I've had people tell me it's different for them. They aren't like me. I may be brave enough and smart enough to manage tenants, but they are not. This is not true. If you know how to generally get along with people, you'll do fine. You are perfectly capable of managing your own tenants. The key is to be pleasant, but firm. You will do your best to make a tenant happy, but only if what the tenant wants will make you happy, too. Never let a tenant run rough-shod over you.

If something they suggest makes you feel uneasy inside, tell them you'll have to think about it and get back to them. Sometimes I have to think something through or talk to other investors before I know how I will respond. It is always scary to have to tell someone no. Tell them why you are saying no. Most people will accept your answer. Remember, your tenants are scared of you, too!

If you get someone who is downright disagreeable, you may want to suggest that they move out before their lease is up. This happened to my sister once. The tenants were always mad at her about this or the other thing. Nothing made them happy. She was glad to let them go early, even if it meant she had to find a new tenant. They were the first tenants she ever actively disliked, and she was eager to replace them with someone nicer.

Most people are really very pleasant and enjoyable to know. You will be exposed to people you never would have met through your normal circle of friends and family. They will teach you new and interesting things. Your life will broaden in ways you didn't expect. Most tenants will recognize a great landlord or landlady when they meet one, and they will go out of their way to get along with you.

So try it. Be your own property manager. It may take years before you are truly comfortable in your new role, but imagine the confidence you will feel. You will have grown as a person. You'll have learned how to manage people, a skill that will stand you in good stead throughout your life. You may surprise yourself by discovering that you actually enjoy interacting with your tenants.

# Chapter Ten

# The Lease

This chapter covers a sample of the types of clauses you could include in your lease. I will discuss each clause individually to explain what it is designed to accomplish and how I approach different tenant responses. The clauses in my leases change over the years as I discover the things my tenants do that I don't want them to do in the future. You will probably also modify your lease as you gain experience.

These clauses will give you a good basis for designing a lease. However, you must have a lawyer who is familiar with the rental laws in your state and city check your lease to make sure it complies with your local requirements and also that it best serves your interest as a property owner. Since I am not an attorney the sample clauses in this chapter are exactly that: samples. It's up to you to get a legal blessing before you use any of them.

This warning also applies to any other comments I make in this chapter when discussing these lease clauses. ALWAYS check with an attorney, especially if you find yourself in a dispute with a tenant, to make sure you are on the right side of the law. Bringing this book to court and reading my opinions to a judge won't adequately protect you.

Developing a relationship with a competent real estate attorney is well worth the investment of time and money. Other investors complain to me that attorneys cost too much. Yes, they do charge a substantial hourly fee, and you need to find one who specializes in real estate if you want the best advice, but it's a good idea to consult with one occasionally. Budget a hundred dollars per year to be spent on legal advice, and then you won't hesitate to call your attorney to double-check your actions. Being frugal is wise, but sometimes it's smart to spend a little money.

You should also read other books which cover leases. You may discover clauses you would like to include in your lease that I do not even mention. No landlady or landlord can include every possible clause in their leases since it would make them so long that tenants would be frightened. Can you imagine their faces if you pulled out a twenty page lease typed on legal sized paper? You will need to compromise, choosing to include those clauses which are most important to you.

When you meet with tenants to have them sign the lease, I highly suggest that you go through your lease clause by clause with them before you let them sign it. This is your last chance to discourage bad tenants who managed to slip through your earlier tenant checks. Good tenants will not object to a strong lease, but bad tenants may suddenly realize that you will expect them to abide by each and every lease clause. If they balk at this point, consider it good riddance of potentially bad tenants.

## My Lease

The lease I use is six pages long plus a signature page printed on regular 8 1/2" by 11" paper. Many model leases provided by housing departments are shorter, and some leases shown as examples in other real estate books are much longer. Indeed, you can buy books devoted entirely to lease clauses. If you are really paranoid, you could make your lease into a small book. I've tried to find a point of moderation where I cover all the necessary agreements without making my lease so long that it scares away tenants.

Because you will probably modify your lease over time, I recommend that you type your lease into a computer so it will be easy to change. I am constantly fiddling with my lease to make it work better for me. You can be sure that the following clauses will have undergone minor revisioning between the time I wrote this book and when you read it.

# General

*This lease is between* _____*, owner(s), and* _____*, tenant(s). It is expressly understood that this agreement is between the owner(s) and each signatory individually and severally. In the event of default by any one signatory, each and every remaining signatory shall be responsible for timely payments of rent and all other provisions of this lease. Use of the singular word 'tenant' shall apply to each named tenant. Use of the word 'owner' shall apply to each named owner.*

When you rent to more than one tenant over the age of eighteen (or twenty-one depending on your state laws), you want every adult to sign the lease. By making each signatory, that is each person who signs the lease, individually responsible for the rent, you are better protected. If sometime in the future you have trouble collecting the rent or a judgement against your tenants, you will only need to find one of the tenants who has money in order to collect it. It will be this tenant's problem to locate the other tenants for reimbursement.

Sometimes two or more single people will want to rent a house together. When you explain to them that they are all individually liable to pay the full rent amount, they may not like this. Why should they pay for Sam's share if Sam disappears or refuses to cough up his portion of the rent?

I'll tell you why. Because they know Sam a lot better than I do. If they don't trust him, then I don't trust him, and they aren't renting this house from me. Everybody signs, or nobody moves in.

Another example would be a married couple who rents your house. If one spouse signs the lease, then later separates from the other spouse and moves out, you would have someone living in your property who does not have a lease with you. This may cause problems if he or she stops paying the rent and you want to evict him or her. It's safest to have both spouses on the lease.

# Leased Premises

*The owner hereby leases to tenant the premises located at*
_____ *which shall include the*
*following:* _____ .

This clause seems clear cut, but you need to pay attention to the inclusions. Items you would never think to list may turn up missing when your tenants move out. Do you have a built-in microwave? List it. Write down its serial number if you want to be 100% exact. Describe the fancy light fixture in the dining room, the drapes and blinds, the computerized thermostat, the keychain remote to the garage door opener, anything that could be easily taken and/or replaced with something less valuable.

A common problem is disappearing drapes. The tenant doesn't intend to steal your drapes. She or he doesn't even like them. The drapes are taken down and replaced with something purchased by the tenant. When the tenant moves, the new drapes go, too. But somehow the old drapes have either been lost or damaged by being stored improperly. The tenant doesn't say anything and hopes you won't notice, or else the tenant plans to say you never had those drapes in the property in the first place. Play it safe. List and describe the drapes in your lease.

# Lease Term

*The term of this lease shall be from* _____ *, 19* _____
*at 12 o'clock noon to* _____ *, 19* _____ *at 12 o'clock
noon.* **Forty-five (45) days written notice to terminate** *at the end
of such term shall be necessary by either party. Upon termination notice given by either party, owner shall then have the right
to hold open houses for prospective replacement tenants or buyers for two (2) hours each Saturday until termination of lease.
The owner shall also have the right to schedule individual showings at other times with four (4) hours notice to current tenant. If
tenant retains possession of the premises after expiration of the
fixed lease term with the permission of the owner, the tenant and
the owner shall continue to be bound by the terms and conditions
of this lease on a month-to-month basis, except for new terms
and conditions which tenant has notice of and agrees to by the
payment of rent.*

I suggest that you specify the exact hour a lease ends. I like
using 12 o'clock noon because one tenant can move out in the
morning while the new tenant moves in that afternoon. Both pay
you rent for that day. I'll admit this doesn't happen often, but it's
nice when it does. My lease specifies that the tenant needs to
give written notice to terminate the lease. Otherwise the lease
will continue on a month-to-month basis.

Despite this, I don't rely on tenants to remember this requirement. Six weeks before the end of their lease I'll talk with
them about their plans. But in case I forget, it is their responsibility to notify me if they want to terminate our agreement. If they
move out at the end of their lease period without giving the required notice, I can charge them for vacancy costs I incur while I
get the property re-rented.

Remember that any time you charge a tenant for causing
you a vacancy, either by breaking the lease early or by neglecting
to give you the required notice that they are moving at the end of

the lease term, you must make a good faith effort to re-rent the property quickly using your normal advertising methods.

If you are lucky enough to re-rent the property immediately, you can't charge your old tenants for vacancy costs you didn't actually incur. However you may charge them for a portion of your advertising expenses. For example, if they break their lease at the halfway mark, you could charge them for half the advertising costs.

When my tenants are signing the lease, I tell them I understand they may need to break the lease early. They may be transferred or may lose a job. (Or a couple may get divorced, but I don't mention this to the tenants). These things happen, and they should tell me as soon as they realize there is a problem. I will work with them to get the property re-rented as quickly as possible so I won't have to charge them for any vacancy. The most I've ever had to charge a tenant was for half a month's rent.

Obviously, the more notice they give you, the better, and in general you'll find new tenants faster if the old tenants move out during the summer months. Other times you will have a rental property in an area which has a strong seasonal rental market such as a ski resort area or a college town.

For example, Boulder is a college town. Students flood the city in August looking for places to live. If someone signs a one year lease with you, but then breaks the lease in January, you may not be able to release the unit for its full rental rate until the following summer. So any loss in rent, that is the difference between the fall rent rate you were receiving and the lower rent you can ask for in mid-winter, can usually be charged to the tenant who breaks the lease early.

Even if you are not renting to students or other seasonal tenants, the fact that other property owners in your area do may become a problem for you. Evictions are handled by the counties in Colorado. A backlog of evictions coming out of one city will affect property owners who are doing an eviction in a different city but in the same county.

This happens in Boulder County. The summer rents are abnormally low in the city of Boulder because many students have left the city. When these rents are raised in August, many students who were paying the low summer rates refuse to move or to pay the winter rent rate. By the end of August the sheriff may have a three week waiting list to send deputies out to handle evictions. A property owner who does an eviction at this time gets in line with the student landlords to schedule an eviction date.

You can find out about local idiosyncracies like this by calling the court that handles evictions in your area. Ask if there is a time of the year when a lot of evictions happen. Then make sure your leases don't end at that time. Your tenants may still choose that month to stop paying rent, especially if they are professional scam artists, but you've done your best to protect yourself.

HINT: Some people recommend attending eviction court to find properties at good prices. Property owners may be emotional at this time and willing to sell to anyone who will make their problem go away. If the discount is good enough, you may want to become the new owner and handle the eviction yourself.

If the owner is still thinking that he or she wants to keep the property, give the owner your card. If the tenant has trashed the property, you may get a call when the owner has a chance to see the damage. I've never personally used this technique, but if you like fixer uppers, you may find a good deal this way.

## Rent

*The total rent for the term of this lease is _____ . The first rent payment in the amount of $ _____ is due on _____, and must be in the form of a cashier's check or money order. If received in the form of a personal check, possession shall be contingent on the check clearing the tenant's bank first. Thereafter, rent is payable in monthly installments of $ _____ each, and shall be made payable to _____, on the _____ day* *of the month unless tenant and owner otherwise agree in writing. If rent is received early, owner will deposit the rent no earlier than the due date. The tenant shall incur a late fee of $20.00 per day for each day the rent is not paid in full. A charge of up to $35.00 may be imposed for any tenant's check returned to owner because of insufficient funds or non-existing account, whether the check is for rent, security deposit, or any other payment. The imposition of such charge shall not preclude a claim for treble damages under C.R.S \*p27 94 21\* 13-21-109. Any late fee and return check charges shall be reasonable estimates of the administrative costs incurred by the owner. Tenant agrees that such costs are difficult to ascertain and that the amounts set forth above are a reasonable measure of liquidated damages.*

I include the total rent for the entire lease period to make it crystal clear that my lease is not a month-to-month lease - it is for the entire lease term. I always insist on the first month's rent and security deposit to be in good-as-cash funds. Can you imagine what a financial disaster it would be to let a tenant move in only to discover later that he or she gave you a bad check? You'll have to evict these tenants with no money to cover the lost rent. Sure, you could try to get a judgement against the tenant, but it may not be worth your time to collect it.

When tenants have trouble coming up with the entire first month's rent plus the security deposit, you may be asked to let them make a partial payment with a second payment coming halfway through the month. If this happens, and you want to rent to these tenants, always collect your security deposit in full and take the rent for a reduced period. If the second half of the rent doesn't appear, you can start eviction proceedings immediately and have a full deposit to protect you.

If instead you agree to wait for the second half of the deposit and it doesn't show up, an eviction judge may think that's not as serious of a problem as non-payment of rent. The judge may order you to agree to a payment plan from the tenant because judges don't like people to be forced out of their homes.While this attitude toward unpaid rent versus unpaid security deposits may or may not be true in your state, I think it's safer to get the deposit up front.

Many leases will say the rent is due on the first, but it's not late until five days later. This has always seemed ridiculous to me. If the rent is due on the first but is not late until the fifth, then when is it really due? On the fifth. My rent is due on the first of the month for all my properties. If someone would prefer a due date of the fifth because that's when he or she gets paid, I don't consider that to be my problem. If they live from paycheck to paycheck, they probably aren't my ideal tenants anyway.

Also, since I collect the rent and pay the mortgages on nine properties, it can get confusing to keep track of who has paid me and which mortgage companies I still have to pay. I want my money on or before the first so I can deposit it all at the same time. If any rent is missing, it's obvious, and I can call my tenants to find out what's happened.

Many tenants think their rent check should arrive exactly on the due date. Heaven forbid that it should arrive early! They don't want to pay their rent until the last possible moment. I point out to them that the lease says I may not deposit a rent check before its due date, then I tell them to send me the rent a week early. They'll avoid late charges (and I'll have the peace of mind that comes from a pile of rent checks waiting to be deposited).

Another option that is extremely popular with my tenants is giving them deposit slips for my business account. My bank has branches in almost every store of a large regional grocery chain. These branches are open until seven o'clock at night. When my tenants belatedly realize it's the first of the month they can dash over to the nearest branch of my bank to deposit their rent. All I have to do is call the automated account information system to verify that my rents have been deposited.

Remember, if you use this method of accepting rent, you must charge different rents for all your properties so you can tell who has or has not deposited their rent. Otherwise if two tenants each owe you $1,000 in rent, but only one deposits a payment, how will you know who you need to call for the missing $1,000? The automated system will only tell you the amount of the deposit, not who made it.

## Payment of Rent by Check

*If mailing rent checks, write on back of check "Payable only to account XXXXXXXXX" to reduce the risk of possible mail fraud.*

If you or your tenants prefer to send checks in the mail, you should protect yourself against mail fraud. In the rural area where I live a ring of thieves hired teenagers to steal checks out of mailboxes and then cash them. In a case like this, who would be liable for the lost money?

I didn't want to find out. I told my tenants I had a new rule. All checks must say on the back "For Deposit Only" with my account number. This means a bank must deposit the checks into my account only. If a bank should ignore this requirement and cash a stolen check instead, the bank would be liable.

Incidentally, I discourage tenants from paying their rent in cash directly to me. If convenience stores keep less than $40 cash in their registers, why would I want to have $1,000 or more in my pocket? I know a landlord who lets his tenants pay him in cash at his office on the first of every month. If I were the receptionist, I would not be very happy about holding that money. We're talking about thousands of dollars. Numerous ex-tenants know how this landlord is paid, and they could have told their friends. I think this landlord is asking for trouble.

If you want your lease to sound official, find out the section of your state law which authorizes you to charge late fees and bad check charges. Include this information in the lease. As you point this section out to your tenants, you will be making it clear that you intend to collect your rent on time and in good funds.

# Utilities

*The tenant shall be responsible for paying for the following utilities or services connected with the property including any transfer fees: _____ . The tenant shall arrange for such utilities or services and for billing directly to tenant to begin upon commencement of this lease. Provision of the payment for utilities and service not listed above shall be the responsibility of the owner. The party responsible for any particular utility or service shall not be liable for failure to furnish the utility or service when the cause of such failure is beyond that party's control.*

I prefer to have my tenants pay for all their utilities. I don't want the hassle of paying multiple bills each month for all of my properties. At one point I reimbursed tenants for water bills in excess of $20 since I wanted them to keep the lawns watered, but tracking how much I owed them was a pain.

Now if I see that a lawn is turning brown, I water it myself and call the tenants when I get home. I politely remind them that it costs a lot of money to resod an entire lawn, and it would require all of their security deposit. I suggest that paying a slightly higher water bill may be more affordable. I also give them a way to save face by saying I understand it's hard to keep up with the watering in a dry state like Colorado, but please keep an eye on the grass. It shouldn't make crunching sounds when they walk across it.

One thing to keep in mind is that in many states unpaid water bills are a lien against the property. In Colorado, for example, if a tenant doesn't pay the water and sewer bill, a lien will be created. When that property is sold, the lien will have to be paid in order for the buyer to get clear title.

Luckily, most water departments have space in their computers for two names and addresses, one for the tenant and one for you. This way you will be notified if the account goes delinquent. If this isn't true in your area, you may have to call to check every few months to make sure your tenants are paying.

Most public service companies can also list both the tenant and the property owner in their billing systems. This is great because even if you forget to get the utilities switched to your name when old tenants move out and new tenants aren't moving in immediately, the public service company will begin billing you automatically when the old tenants' service terminates.

# Use

*The property shall be used as a residence with no more than _____ persons, and for no other purpose without the prior written consent of the owner. Occupancy by guests without prior written consent staying over ten (10) days within one calendar month will be considered to be in violation of this clause. If it is determined that one or more additional tenants have occupied the premises, such unauthorized tenants shall cause the rent for the premises to increase by $5.00 per day for each unauthorized tenant for each day exceeding the allowable ten (10) days. Owner may, but is not obligated to, give written consent to allow the new tenants to continue occupying the property with an additional security deposit of $ _____ and with the increase in rent as described above. A newborn or adopted child shall not be deemed an additional tenant.*

There are no clear federal guidelines for property owners to use when setting a maximum number of people to allow in a given property. Sometimes there are local regulations such as the one in Boulder which says only three unrelated people may live in a rental unit. If a regulation like this exists in your area, you'll probably be okay if you comply.

Many areas don't have an occupancy regulation. What do you do then? Can you say only so many people per square foot or one person per bedroom? Following arbitrary rules like these may get you into trouble. For example, a single parent has sued and won the right to live in a one bedroom unit with a child of the opposite sex. Though HUD, the federal department of housing, uses square foot guidelines, they have said that these guidelines are not for general use.

Some groups such as Oxford House have sued municipalities over laws which restrict the number of unrelated people in a house. Oxford House rents houses with numerous bedrooms and subleases them to groups of recovering alcoholics. These people often need inexpensive places to live because their past problems with alcohol have damaged their finances. Oxford House also believes they need group support to stay sober. Recovered alcoholics are considered handicapped; this means they are a federally protected class. You can see the conflicting issues here.

In addition some areas of the country which have experienced large influxes of Hispanic immigrants have enacted laws restricting the people who may live in a home to immediate family members. Uncles and aunts and cousins are not allowed. A suit was filed that these limitations were discriminatory because, intentionally or unintentionally, Hispanics who have broader definitions of immediate family were being disproportionately affected by the new regulations.

If you want a way to restrict how many people can live in your property, you should definitely discuss your options with a lawyer who is familiar with your local laws. And whatever rules you decide to use, be consistent. You don't want to get into trouble for treating some people differently than others.

# Pets

*No pets shall be brought on the property without prior written consent of the owner. Any damages caused by pets shall not be considered normal and reasonable wear and tear whether or not the tenant has obtained written consent. Tenant agrees to pay any additional security deposit or monthly rent increases charged as a result of having a pet. Such extra charges shall not be construed as waiving any right owner may have to damages or security deposit(s) as a result of damages to the premises caused by pets.*

I do generally allow pets. For more information on this topic, look in Chapter Eight, Qualifying Potential Tenants.

## House and Neighborhood Rules

*If the leased property is part of a multiple unit building or complex, tenant agrees to comply with all regulations now or hereinafter made by the owner or the building complex management relating to the leased property and any common grounds. The regulations, if any, shall be attached to this lease. If this property is located in a neighborhood with covenants, tenants agree to follow these covenants and are liable for any penalties if they do not. A copy of the covenants is included with this lease. In addition tenants agree to abide by any federal, state, or local laws.*

If you own a duplex or apartment building, you want your tenants to obey the community rules. If your unit is a condominium or townhouse, you want to let the tenants know what the rules are for the complex as a whole. Even single family homes are subject to covenants and city regulations. For example, if the homeowners association or the city decides to hire someone to weed your property's yard because your tenants haven't, you want to make it clear that the tenants are financially liable for this bill.

When I reach this part of the lease, I mention those rules which I think are the ones most likely to cause problems. Many of my properties are in cities where snow must be shoveled off sidewalks within twenty-four hours or the city will charge the property owner to have the city do it instead. I remind my tenants to make arrangements with a neighbor or friend if they plan to be out of town during the winter.

# Subordination

*This lease shall be subordinate to all existing and future mort-gages and deeds of trust upon the property. If a mortgage holder becomes the owner of the property by foreclosure, tenant agrees to be bound by this lease to the mortgage holder.*

If case a future lender requires that a lease must be subordi-nate before you can refinance, you'll want to have this clause in your lease. You want to make sure you have the option to refi-nance your properties without having to get your tenants to sign a subordination release. Most tenants would cooperate, but what if you've got one who's ornery and decides you should pay them to sign a release? It's better to avoid this potential problem.

# Entry and Inspection

*Tenant shall permit owner or owner's agent to enter the premises at reasonable times and upon reasonable notice for the purpose of making necessary or convenient repairs and/or improvements, or to show the premises to prospective tenants, buyers or mort-gagees. Reasonable notice shall be defined as at least four hours notice in non-emergency situations. Unless tenant agrees other-wise, entry times shall be limited to 9:00 am to 7:00 pm. In addi-tion tenants shall have the right to change the locks, but must provide the owner with copies of keys in advance of installation.*

When a tenant rents a property, he or she has a leasehold on that property. This means that you have to obtain the tenant's permission in most situations in order to enter the property. In general, you should not enter the property without giving prior notice to your tenant unless it is a bona fide emergency.

One landlady told me how she and her husband dropped by a rental property they owned. I don't know whether they gave notice to their tenant, but they did enter the property. And what did they find? A leaking pipe under the kitchen sink. Water on the loose can be extremely damaging, so they immediately proceeded to work on fixing the leak.

The tenant returned home before they had finished the repair and told them to leave. They refused to go because their lease allowed them to make repairs. The tenant called the police, and to their surprise, the property owners were escorted out.

Even though they had the right to evict their tenant for breaking a key clause of the lease, they didn't have the right to enter the property in the meantime. Their two options were to reason gently with the tenant or to proceed with an eviction to enforce their right to enter the property for the purpose of doing repairs.

I do allow my tenants to change the locks because it is a legitimate security concern that the previous tenants and their friends may have made copies of the keys. However, tenants tend to forget the requirement to provide new keys to the property owner. They mean to do it, but never get around to actually sending a key. You may want to check your keys when you visit your properties to make sure they still work.

# Indemnification

*Owner shall not be liable for any damage or injury which is incurred by tenant or any other person or damage to tenant's personal possessions on the property or in common areas thereof. The tenant shall not hold the owner liable for any injury or damage resulting from worn or defective wiring or by the breaking, freezing or stoppage of the sewage or plumbing; furthermore, tenant agrees to assume the risk of injury to tenant, tenant's family or guests arising from slipping or falling in the common passageways, parking lot or other general areas, whether or not these areas are kept free from snow, ice and water. The tenant agrees to indemnify and hold the owner harmless for and against any and all liability arising from injury during the term of this lease to person or property, caused wholly or in part by any act or omission of tenant, or of tenant's guests, employees, or assigns of tenant.* **Tenant acknowledges that tenant is responsible for obtaining renter's insurance to cover tenant's personal belongings if such coverage is desired.** *Tenant also acknowledges that some renter's insurance includes liability coverage for the tenant in case the property is accidentally damaged.*

This is another clause which may or may not protect me in court depending on the circumstances, but I figure it doesn't hurt to include it. Of course, if I've done something negligent such as fail to have an older furnace inspected, and my tenants suffer from carbon monoxide poisoning, I will be liable no matter what I put in the lease. This clause is designed primarily to protect me from liability for foolish or careless behavior on the part of my tenants and their guests.

Renter's insurance is prudent for both you and your tenants. For more information on this topic, refer to Chapter Nine, Day to Day Details.

You should also give thought to liability insurance for yourself. Even if you try to be the best and most conscientious of all property owners, things happen. Some real estate experts will tell you to incorporate or form trusts to protect yourself. After talking with a couple of lawyers I've decided it's more cost effective to have good liability insurance policies.

In addition to the landlord liability insurance included as part of my landlord property coverage for each rental house, I have also purchased an umbrella liability policy. My decision to handle potential liability in this manner is a personal one, and you should make your own inquiries before deciding what approach would be best for you.

## Possession

*If the owner is unable to deliver possession of the property at the commencement of this lease, the owner shall not be liable for any damage caused thereby, nor shall this agreement be void or voidable. However, neither shall the tenant be liable for any rent until possession is delivered. Tenant may terminate this agreement if possession is not delivered within ten (10) days of the commencement of the term hereof. Possession is contingent on the first month's rent and security deposit being received in Colorado good funds or clearing the tenant's bank if presented in the form of a check.*

I'm always amazed when tenants breeze right by this clause despite my explanation of exactly what it means. If my old tenants don't move out on time, my new tenants are still bound by the lease they've signed with me. And I'm not liable to cover their hotel costs or any other damages they may experience while waiting the ten days!

Even if a tenant did protest, I would never allow myself to become liable for any of their expenses should I be unable to deliver possession. I do intend in good faith to provide possession per the lease we signed, but whether the current tenants move out when their lease is up is beyond my control.

However, I would be willing to reduce the ten days to zero if it were important to a prospective tenant. After all, most tenants will have trouble finding another property quickly. By the time they find a second rental that suits them, I may have gotten the old tenants out. Since the new tenants have already gone through the application process with me, it may be faster and easier for them to resign a lease with me even if the old one expired due to lack of immediate possession.

I never give possession to tenants before I have their security deposit and first month's rent in good as cash funds. It's not enough to deposit a personal check into my account. I may get a notice from my bank two weeks later announcing that the check bounced. At that point my tenants will have lived in the property free for half a month, and I will have no security deposit to cover my losses while I evict them.

Usually I require tenants to give me a cashier's check. This can be a problem if they have flown into town to get a rental in advance of a move to the area. Here's how I handle that situation. As soon as I've run a credit check on them and have notified them that I've accepted them, I expect the tenants to two-day airmail their cashier's check to me. Or they can do a direct deposit from their bank account into mine. At a minimum I need to promptly receive the security deposit to hold a property for someone. And the first month's rent is payable in good funds before I'll give possession.

While I'm waiting for the cashier check, I'll fax a lease for the tenants to sign. They can either airmail it back with their cashier's check, or we can include a clause stating that we agree fax signatures will be considered legal and binding. That way we can handle everything over the phone lines or through a shipping service. Remember to go over the lease with your new tenants over the phone. You always want to make sure they understand what they are signing.

# Default

*If the tenant shall fail to pay rent when due, or breaches the terms of this lease in any other way, after written notice of such default given in the manner required by law the owner at owner's option may terminate all rights of tenant hereunder. If the tenant abandons or vacates the property after failing to pay rent, the owner may consider any personal possessions left on the property to be abandoned and may dispose of them in any manner allowed by law. In the event the owner reasonably believes that such abandoned possessions have no value, they may be discarded. All possessions on the property not excepted by law are hereby subject to lien in favor of owner for the payment of all sums due hereunder. If owner asserts dominion over any possessions considered abandoned, owner shall be considered to be without knowledge that tenant does not intend to abandon these possessions unless tenant gives owner written notification. Owner shall provide tenant with a written list of all possessions over which dominion has been asserted.*

What happens when you evict a tenant for not paying rent, and that tenant still has a bunch of stuff in your unit? Do you have to store it? Can you sell it? How can you protect yourself against being sued later for throwing out a supposedly valuable antique when all you saw was a broken lamp?

Laws vary state by state on how default situations can be handled. You should check with a real estate attorney to find out your state's laws, but you'll want to address in the lease whether you may throw stuff away or sell it. A house full of stuff is unrentable, so you need to make sure you can get rid of it somehow. Storing it may not be a good idea. Besides costing you money, the tenants may claim their property was damaged while in your care and possession. These types of arguments with tenants will cost you in time, enthusiasm, and possibly money.

# Real Estate Agent

*Tenant acknowledges that the owner or owner's spouse is a licensed real estate agent in the state of _____, and can be assumed to have an above average knowledge of real estate matters. The owner rents properties with the expressed intent to make a profit.*

If you are an agent, you may rent a property to some clients while they are looking for a home to buy. This could get you into trouble. If you are working for them as a fiduciary agent, doesn't that mean their interests must come first? Is it okay for their agent to make a profit by renting them a house? To prevent any misunderstandings, it's best to include a clause like this one which clarifies your relationship and your responsibilities to your client.

# Bills Immediately Due and Payable

*Tenant acknowledges that owner may be billed by the city for tenant's failure to remove snow from public sidewalks within twenty-four hours or failure to maintain yard in a condition to satisfy city or home owner association requirements. Owner may also be billed for unpaid water bills or may incur charges related to the repair of damage caused by the tenant. When owner bills the tenant for reimbursement of these fees, that bill shall be payable within ten days. If any bill is not paid to owner within ten days of receipt by tenant, tenant will have breached this lease and eviction may occur at the owner's option. Tenant agrees that the owner is not obligated to use any portion of the security deposit to pay these fees and expenses.*

It's possible that a tenant will cost you money while occupying your property. You'll want to have the right to be reimbursed for any out-of-pocket expenses without having to rely solely on the security deposit. Otherwise it is possible that by the end of the lease the tenant will owe you more than what you've received as a security deposit. Water bills can add up fast! A clause like this allows you to demand your money immediately while you still have a full security deposit.

# Security Deposit

*The tenant shall pay the owner the sum of $ _____ as a security deposit to secure the performance of this lease. Of this amount, $ _____ has already been paid, and its receipt is hereby acknowledged. The remainder shall be paid by: _____ . The security deposit shall be paid by cashier's check or money order. If paid by personal check, possession of property is contingent on funds clearing the tenant's bank first. The security deposit may not be used by the tenant in lieu of rent. The owner shall within sixty (60) days after the termination of this lease or* *the surrender and acceptance of the premises, whichever occurs last, return the security deposit to the tenant or provide the tenant with a written statement as to why any portion of the security deposit was retained. The owner shall be deemed to have given prior notice for the retention of any of the deposit by mailing the statement to the last known address of each tenant. Any refund shall be divided equally between each tenant signing this lease unless the tenants provide the owner with a written agreement signed by all tenants which states otherwise. At the expiration of the lease term, the tenant shall surrender the premises, including any furniture, appliances, outside area, yards and driveways required to be maintained under this lease, in as good state and condition as received, **including a professional truck mounted cleaning of all carpeting with a receipt provided to owner**, and shall pay the owner a reasonable charge for the costs of any cleaning as may be necessary to fulfill this duty if such cleaning is not performed by the tenant.  The tenant expressly agrees that the security deposit secures the performance of this maintenance and cleaning obligation, and that the deposit may be used at the option of the owner to pay such charges, including reasonable labor. The owner shall have the option to use the security deposit during the term of this lease to fulfill obligations of the tenant under this lease. The owner reserves the right to turn security deposits over to a successor property owner.*

I point out to my tenants when we review the lease that the security deposit is not the same as the last month's rent. Some landlords recommend that the security amount never be the same amount as the rent in order to make the difference clear. In Texas where I currently can't demand a security deposit as large as the monthly rent and still find a tenant, this issue is moot. In Colorado I charge the same amount for both the monthly rent and the security deposit.

However, I believe my lease is quite clear on the distinction since it states that the security deposit may not be used by the tenant in lieu of rent. Even if a tenant later claims that I did not verbally discuss this, it is in the signed lease.

When refunding security deposits, you will be under pressure from the tenant to return the full amount as soon as possible. I've done this twice in my life, and each time I've regretted it. Additional expenses or damage to the property later became apparent. Since I had already returned the deposits in full, I had to swallow the expenses without compensation.

In Colorado landlords automatically have by law the right to hold security deposits for up to thirty days. This time period can be lengthened to a maximum of sixty days if this is put into the lease. You should use the maximum amount of time allowed in your area. I assure my tenants that I will refund their deposits as quickly as possible, but I warn them that I put sixty days in my lease for several reasons.

First, it may take time to discover how much it will cost to repair certain types of damage. And second, I may have a personal emergency that prevents me from assessing any damage and its cost immediately. For example, I or close family members may be sick and in the hospital.

If I have tenants who are planning to buy a house at the end of their lease, I may agree to do a walk-through of the rental property before they go to the closing on their house. If everything looks okay, I may, at my discretion, refund part of their security deposit immediately. But I will never refund the entire amount until after they have moved out. I've been burned twice. I don't intend to get burned a third time.

Always provide a written list of any charges you are making against a tenant's security deposit. Usually you will not be allowed to charge for your own time spent fixing or cleaning the property unless you provide for this in the lease. A friend of mine does exactly this, setting a charge for his time of $20 per hour. Since I don't want to end up in an argument with any tenant over whether I spent an appropriate amount of time doing repairs or cleaning, I don't do this.

Instead I handle most light cleaning myself without charge. If the property needs a deep cleaning, I hire a cleaning service. Their fee can be charged against the security deposit so it doesn't cost me any money, and I can't be accused of inflating the time in order to profit personally.

To prevent an argument with the tenant about the condition of the property, you should do a walk-through with the tenant after the tenant has moved out and you've had a chance to assess the damages. If you live in a water lien state, be sure to check the water bill due on the date the lease ends. And, incidentally, don't forget to get all the utilities switched back into your name if you don't have it set up to happen automatically.

When you have a new tenant moving in as soon as the old tenant moves out, you'll have to do your walk-through that same day. Overall, it becomes difficult to determine who was responsible for what damage when you don't experience any real vacancy for years in a row. In situations like this, I tend to be fairly lenient. How can I complain about $200 in damages when I haven't had any costly vacancies in a long time?

The distinction between normal wear and tear and damage can be a matter of opinion. Once, when my father was at small claims court waiting for his case to come up, he observed as the judge decided a case between a tenant and landlord. The landlord had withheld money from the security deposit because the dining room carpet had red stains. The tenant claimed this was normal wear and tear when living with children. The landlord said she should have protected the carpet or else not served colored drinks to her children.

In this case the judge agreed with the landlord, but I can easily imagine the decision going the other way. Since many states provide for expensive penalties against a property owner who wrongfully withholds money from a deposit, I am very careful in this area. If you are really paranoid about tenants falsely claiming that the property was in bad condition when they moved in, you can take instant pictures of your new tenants standing in the property after they sign the lease, or you can videotape them as you go through the house with them. Comment verbally on the condition of each room if your machine handles sound. A video-tape like this would be strong ammunition in the court room.

Currently I'm not this cautious. I've had tenants damage blinds and lose drapes. I've had them destroy a small area of grass in the backyard where they set up a playhouse for their kid. And some tenants have left my houses in less than pristine states of cleanliness. It's amazing what I've found underneath stoves. But unless the problems start to add up to a significant amount, at least $200, I rarely deduct anything from the security deposits.

I can be especially forgiving if the tenants have fixed other problems the house had for which they were not responsible. In one of my houses a railing pulled away from the wall because the house shifted, and I was very glad to have the tenant figure out how to solve that problem. I was then willing to overlook some minor damage caused by that tenant.

On the other hand, most tenants won't argue about a few deductions. As long as they get back most of their money, they aren't interested in arguing with you any more than you want to argue with them. So I'm getting pickier as I get more experi-enced.

When you do return the security deposit, it's important to give it to the right person. You may not know your tenants are getting a divorce, but if you return the deposit to one spouse, the other may not get his or her share. Or if you have two or more singles sharing the rental, paying one of them may not be a good idea. If someone else doesn't get her or his money, you may wind up paying twice. It will be your problem to get back the extra money from the first person you paid. Good luck. It's better to avoid this possible problem by cutting separate checks.

One place where I explicitly define how clean the property should be is for the carpets. I provide properties that have clean carpet when tenants move in and I expect the carpets to be in the same state of cleanliness when they move out. I do not want the tenants to rent a carpet cleaning machine from the local supermarket. A truck mounted system does a far superior job, and that's what I expect. It's a good idea to remind tenants about this requirement when either you or they give notice to terminate.

The last paragraph of the security deposit clause states that I may use this deposit to cover any tenant obligations. This mean that the deposit covers unpaid rent as well as any damage to the property.

## Assignment and Subletting

*Tenant shall not assign this agreement or sublet any portion of the property without prior written consent of the owner.*

I insist on choosing my own tenants. While I will consider new tenants who are recommended by old tenants who want to break a lease, they must meet my standards. I want to interview them and run a credit report. The one exception I may make occurs when not all of the old tenants are leaving.

For example, three young men rented one of my properties. As I expected, one of them eventually fell in love and wanted to set up a new home. The lease term would not be up for many months, but he had a friend who wanted to take his place in the house and on the lease. I signed a new lease with the two remaining tenants plus the new tenant without running a credit check on him. Since the other two had been good tenants for over a year and a half and each would remain fully liable for the total rent, I felt my risk was low.

## Maintenance, Repairs or Alterations

*The tenant acknowledges that the property is in good order and repair unless otherwise indicated in this lease or in an attached inspection report. Tenant shall at tenant's expense maintain the property in a clean and sanitary manner including floor and wall surfaces, appliances, and the yard and shall surrender the property at the end of this lease in as good condition as received, ordinary and reasonable wear and tear excepted. Tenant acknowledges that repairs may have to be made to the property during the tenant's leasehold, and tenant is not due any decrease in rent if repairs are made within a reasonable time period by owner. Tenant shall be responsible for all repairs caused by tenant's negligence and by tenant's family or guests. Tenant shall not paint, paper or otherwise redecorate or make alterations to the property without prior written consent of the owner. Tenant shall be responsible for the following outside maintenance:* _____ .

My tenants are responsible for watering the lawn and gardens, shoveling snow from the public sidewalks, and basic weeding. I do try to visit each of my properties in the early spring when the weeds are first taking off. I'll spend half a day working on each yard, getting it into good shape.

Besides showing my tenants how I expect the yard to look, I get a chance to study the exterior of the house. Does the deck need to be stained again? Should I touch up the paint on the house trim? Do any of the bushes or trees need pruning? The better maintained my properties are, the more pride the tenants will have in their homes. They'll take greater care of my house, and this results in a higher property value for me.

# Waiver

*Any waiver by either party, or any breach of any clause of this lease, shall not be considered to be a continuing waiver of a subsequent breach of the same or a different clause of this lease. Any acceptance of a partial payment of rent by owner shall not be deemed a waiver of owner's right to the full amount thereof nor waiver of owner's right to begin eviction proceedings.*

You may decide to ignore a clause of your lease. Perhaps a new pet shows up or a girlfriend moves in. Since the property is being well maintained, you look the other way. Whatever clause it is that you decide to ignore, you want the rest of the lease to still be in force.

In case a tenant is late with the rent, you may want the option to accept partial payment while making it clear that the rest of the rent is still due and its nonpayment is cause for eviction. Laws regarding how evictions are handled vary state by state, and you should check with a lawyer before taking partial rent.

# Severability

*The unenforceability of any clause of this lease shall not effect the enforceability of any other clause or clauses.*

Severability comes into play when someone, presumably a judge, decides one clause or section of a clause in a lease is not legal. If this happens to you, you'll want the rest of the lease to remain in force.

# Attorney's Fees

*If either party to this lease prevails in any legal action brought by either party to enforce the terms hereof or relating to the property, the prevailing party shall NOT be entitled to reimbursement for all costs incurred in connection with such action including reasonable attorney's fees. Each party will be responsible for their own costs including attorney's fees.*

I used to have this clause award attorney's fees to the prevailing party since I thought it would deter a tenant from dragging me into court. But on second thought, I don't always agree with the verdicts of judges. It would be bad enough to lose a case; I don't want to add insult to injury by making myself liable for my tenant's costs if they win. What an awful thought!

Some property owners may consider making only the tenant liable for the winner's legal costs. If the tenant wins a case, the owner doesn't have to pay for the tenant's costs, but if the owner wins, the tenant must reimburse the owner's costs.

Clever thought, but it has a problem. Judges don't like leases which don't treat parties equally. The judge will likely say whoever wins will have costs reimbursed if the property owner has reserved that right solely for himself or herself.

Since I don't like that idea, I'm back to each party paying for separate costs, win or lose. At least that way I can limit how much I choose to spend on a case. I'd hate to be responsible for some tenant's inflated bill.

# Notice

*Any notice which either party may or is required to give, may be given by mailing the notice to tenant at the property and to owner at _____ . Notice to one tenant shall be deemed notice to all tenants. A change of address to be used for notification purposes shall be effective only if notice is given in writing.*

It may seem silly to send a notice to your property after a tenant has moved out, but you need to have somewhere to send notices to your tenants. It is the tenant's responsibility to provide a forwarding address to the post office. Indeed, if you ever win a judgement against a tenant and want to find out where they moved, you should remember this tidbit: for a small fee, the post office will give you that new address.

# Yard Maintenance

*Tenants are responsible for mowing and watering the lawn, and watering other landscape plants. Tenants are not allowed to apply pesticides or herbicides to the yard without the written con-*

*sent of the owner. Under NO circumstances barring an emer-*
*gency shall the tenant prune, cut down, or destroy any plants on*
*the property. If tenant violates the conditions of this clause, ten-*
*ant shall be liable for any cost incurred in decontaminating the*
*soil and/or the cost of replacement plants and installation.*

This clause is more specific than most you might see regarding yard maintenance. My caution here is based on some
experience. I once lived across the street from a house formerly
owned by a man who worked for a local city. His job included
spraying weeds. He brought home some serious herbicide which
needed to be diluted, but he applied it full strength to his yard.
The man sold the house. Trees in the yard and in neighboring
yards started to sicken.

What did the new owner have to do when he determined
what the old owner had done? The yard's dirt had to be removed
to a depth of four feet and disposed of as toxic waste. While this
example may be extreme, nationwide homeowners misuse and
overuse both pesticides and herbicides. Toxic waste situations
are not good for property values. Tenants must get written permission from me to use any poisons on my properties.

Regarding my concern over pruning, I once bought a house
partially because I loved the front yard. In particular I was enam-
ored of some bushes. One day when I came by, I was shocked to
see those bushes gone. I kept my cool fairly well when I knocked
on the door and asked my tenant what had happened. It turned
out he didn't want the bushes blocking the front window, but I
learned my lesson. Landscaping affects the value of a property to
a great extent, and I want to be the only one who makes major
pruning decisions.

## Additional Terms and Conditions

Though this section has many more lines in my actual lease, I have shortened it for this book. I write down details here about any pets I have agreed to accept. It's also a good place to list phone numbers for both the tenant and the owner.

## Entire Agreement

*The foregoing six pages constitute the entire agreement between the parties and may be modified only in writing signed by both parties. The following exhibits, if any, have been made a part of this agreement before the parties' execution hereof: _____ . The undersigned tenant(s) hereby acknowledge receipt of a copy hereof.*

*Dated this day of _____ , 19 _____ .*

*Owner: _____ Owner: _____*

*Tenant: _____ Tenant: _____*

You should mention how many pages are in your lease so a tenant can't say you've inserted a page he or she never saw before. In addition, it's a good idea to have the tenants initial all other pages to prove that those are the pages they read. This may seem a little paranoid since I've never landed in court, thank God, but better safe than sorry.

My lease is by no means exhaustive. Its length is a compromise between caution and my desire not to scare off prospective tenants. It is constantly evolving as my tenants teach me where I need to be more specific. Your lease will also change as you learn what does and does not matter to you. The area of the country where you live may also dictate adding clauses to handle special local circumstances.

# Chapter Eleven

# 1031 Tax Deferred Exchanges

The Congress of the United States has done several things to make investing in real estate attractive from a tax viewpoint. Besides allowing small investors to depreciate their properties, the government has also provided a way for investors to switch their investments from one property to another on a tax deferred basis.

Section 1031 of the Internal Revenue Code (IRC) and regulations issued by the Internal Revenue Service have established and clarified the tax exchange rules which allow investors to sell one or more properties and to buy replacement properties without triggering the usual capital gain tax consequences of a sale. Properties involved in a 1031 tax deferred exchange must be "like kind" which means real property for real property. Land, apartment buildings, houses, attached housing such as townhomes and condominiums, and commercial properties such as office buildings and strip malls are all considered real property.

This provision in our tax code gives real estate investors a wonderful opportunity to improve or relocate their portfolios of investment properties. If you think that you could make more money or save time owning a different property, you can sell the one you have and buy the better one without losing part of your investment to the tax man (though you will still have other typical closing costs).

Compare this to what happens when you invest in the stock market. Let's say your stock rises dramatically in value, but you think it won't do as well in the future. If you sell it, you'll have to pay taxes on your gain before you can reinvest what's left of your money.

The sale of investment real estate works differently. If you correctly follow the 1031 tax exchange rules, you can buy and sell properties without triggering any federal taxes due. In addition most states will consider 1031 tax deferred sales non-taxable events. Nevertheless, due to the differences between state tax laws, you should check with your accountant to verify how your state views 1031 tax deferred exchanges.

## Personal Residence Versus Investment Property

The rules for doing a tax free exchange for investment properties are different than the rules for selling a personal residence. A personal home tax exemption happens almost automatically. As long as your gain is $250,000 or less if you are a single person, or $500,000 or less if you are a married couple, and you have owned and used your home as your primary residence for at least two out of the last five years, you won't owe any capital gain taxes.

If you want the sale of your investment property to qualify for a 1031 tax deferred exchange, however, you will have to meet a number of requirements. If, like most investors, you are not exchanging one property directly for another property, you must hire what is called a "qualified intermediary" to hold your money between the time you sell one property and buy a new property. This intermediary will help you complete the required paperwork and make sure you follow the rules correctly.

If you don't comply exactly with the Internal Revenue Service regulations, your exchange may not be considered valid. You will owe capital gain taxes even if you have reinvested your money into another real estate investment.

## To Exchange or Not

Some people think they will never do a 1031 tax deferred exchange. They intend to buy their target value of properties and hold these properties until the loans are paid off. They want to avoid the costs of selling a property which may include sales commissions, potential vacancy, and miscellaneous closing costs. These buy and hold investors also want to avoid the hassle of selling properties.

Despite the disadvantages inherent in selling an investment property, many situations may arise which would make a 1031 tax deferred exchange desirable. You should be familiar with how the rules work because if you are a real estate investor for very long, you will likely encounter a situation where you'll want to use a tax deferred exchange.

## Why You May Want to Sell Your Property

Despite the costs involved in selling a property, sometimes it makes more sense to get out of a specific investment and into a different one. Perhaps the neighborhood where your property is located has become undesirable, causing you a number of difficulties. Vacancies may have become harder to fill, you may be concerned about your safety when visiting the property, and your potential to experience appreciation on your investment has decreased.

Even if you still like the neighborhood around your property, you may decide to move to a different city or state. Americans are a famously mobile people. If you buy properties in Illinois, then decide to retire in Oklahoma to be near your relatives, you will have a problem. Either you must hire a property manager to take care of your investments for you when you move, or else you will need a way to take your investments with you.

Some people exchange in order to consolidate their real estate holdings. Let's say you own five condominiums. You may decide to sell them and trade the equity into a small apartment complex, or, conversely, you may own an apartment house and hate it. You may want to trade into single family homes instead.

---

Sometimes gaining control of family property will encourage you to make a 1031 tax deferred exchange. After his grandfather's death, a friend of mine and his sister were left with joint ownership of some farm land in Missouri. Since the property was producing a cash flow rate of return which was less than 2% per year, the siblings decided to sell the property.

Because of the way the grandfather had structured his estate, actually putting his grandchildren on the title to the land many years ago, the grandson's taxable gain in his inheritance was almost the full value of his share of the property. If he sold it in the normal fashion, he would owe tens of thousands in taxes.

He used a 1031 tax deferred exchange instead so he could avoid paying taxes at the time of sale. He reinvested his share of the sale proceeds in a single family house in Colorado. This house was located close to his personal home so it would be easy for him to manage, and it promised a much higher rate of return.

---

If you have purchased properties with a partner, you may reach a point where you would like to dissolve the partnership. Whether you sell out your interest in the joint properties to your partner, or together you decide to sell the property on the open market, you'll want a way to take your full equity with you without letting the tax man take a bite. Even if your partner plans to keep his or her share in cash and pay taxes on it, you can still use a 1031 tax deferred exchange to shelter your share of the proceeds.

Another reason you may decide to do a tax deferred exchange is because you need to pull money out of a property, but you can't qualify to refinance. Or the refinance won't pull out as much cash as you need. In this case it's possible to sell the property, deduct the selling costs, pay taxes on the money you take out, and reinvest the rest on a tax deferred basis. This way you can postpone paying taxes on the money you want to keep invested in real estate.

---

Don't rely blindly on an attorney, certified public accountant, or title company employee to explain the 1031 tax deferred exchange rules to you correctly. Unless this person has been trained in real estate tax laws and specializes in exchanges, he or she may not understand all the rules.

For example, a real estate broker in Colorado needed to sell his four-plex in order to get some much needed cash. The broker didn't need all of the proceeds from the sale, but when he checked with an attorney, he was told 1031 tax deferred exchanges are an all or nothing deal. The attorney said if the broker kept and spent any of the money, he wasn't allowed to reinvest the rest on a tax deferred basis. THIS IS NOT TRUE.

The broker could have used an exchange to protect some of his money. Unfortunately, he was given incorrect advice and didn't do a 1031 tax deferred exchange. He paid taxes on the full amount of gain, leaving him with less to reinvest after he took out the amount he needed to cover his immediate cash requirements.

---

A parent may exchange properties for the purposes of estate planning. If a parent owns one large apartment building and knows that his two children cannot agree on anything, he may decide to sell his building and exchange the proceeds into two buildings. Then he could leave one building to each child separately, preventing future co-ownership squabbles.

Or someone with a large apartment building may want to liquidate his or her investment over a period of time. By exchanging into many smaller properties, this investor can sell one unit at a time as funds are desired.

These are just some of the reasons why people who want to stay invested in real estate may find themselves exchanging property. The main objective is to keep your hands on as much of your money as you can. If you pay some of it to the government you will have less to reinvest. Less to reinvest means you will have to wait longer before you achieve your financial goals.

## Taxable Gain

The reason to do a 1031 tax deferred exchange is so you can defer paying taxes on your gain in a property or properties. Obviously you must have a gain to protect from taxes before it makes sense to participate in an exchange. If you have a small gain, the costs of a 1031 tax deferred exchange may be more than you could save in taxes. And if you have a loss you certainly don't want to pay for an exchange.

A simple exchange of one property for another property currently costs about $500 for the intermediary's services. If you are exchanging from one property into two or more properties, the fee will go up $250 or so for each additional property. Sometimes you will also be charged miscellaneous fees for items such as long distance phones calls, faxes, overnight services, and copies. Get a complete list of probable costs from whomever you plan to use as your qualified intermediary so you can estimate the total cost of doing an exchange. Any exchange costs you incur can be deducted as additional selling costs.

Since you will decide to do an exchange only if the amount you'll save from taxes will be more than the cost of doing the exchange, you must first determine how much your potential tax liability will be. Calculating the amount of taxable gain for a property can get complicated. You will need to know several numbers: your selling price, your selling costs, and your adjusted basis in the property. Let's take a look at these three areas.

### Selling Price

You probably have a good idea of your property's value. You've been receiving flyers in the mail from real estate agents who have sold other properties in the neighborhood and you've been calling on "For Sale" signs to find out asking prices. Agents can show you the sold prices for properties like the one you want to sell. And you can always pay for an appraisal.

### Selling costs

Selling costs involve a number of fees such as real estate commissions and title insurance. Most agents will do a net sheet for you which lists all of the costs which will have to be subtracted from your sale proceeds. If you don't plan to use an agent, a title company or a lawyer who specializes in assisting For Sale by Owners may give you an idea of what fees to expect.

Your "amount realized" is what you get after subtracting the selling costs from the selling price. Many sellers will then subtract the balance of any loans on the property to get their net proceeds. Many sellers think that the amount of money they walk away with at closing is their taxable gain, but this isn't true. The Internal Revenue Service ignores loans. We'll see why later in this chapter.

For now, to find out your taxable gain, subtract the selling costs from the anticipated selling price, but then also subtract your "adjusted basis" in the property instead of your loan balances. The resulting number is the gain on which you will potentially owe taxes.

# Adjusted Basis

Your adjusted basis is the purchase price you paid plus the closing costs for that purchase plus the cost of capital improvements you made while you owned the property, minus the depreciation you took over the years.

**Adjusted basis = Purchase price + purchase closing costs + capital improvement costs - accumulated depreciation**

Let's say you purchased an investment house ten years ago for $100,000 and you paid $2,000 in closing costs. Your beginning basis in the property was $102,000. You've owned the property for ten years.

Based on the tax assessor's valuation when you bought the property, you decided ten years ago that 85% of the property's purchase price came from the value of the improvements, not the land. Eighty-five percent of $100,000 (some closing costs may also be depreciated) was $85,000. Dividing $85,000 by 27.5 years gave you a $3,000 annual depreciation expense.

Since you've owned the property for ten years, the $3,000 annual depreciation adds up to a total depreciation expense of $30,000. Your beginning basis in your investment property was $102,000. Subtracting the $30,000 you've taken in depreciation gives you $72,000. If you've made no improvements to the property, your adjusted basis is $72,000.

| | |
|---|---|
| **Purchase price** | **$100,000** |
| **Closing cost** | **$2,000** |
| **Beginning basis** | **$102,000** |
| **Yearly depreciation** | **$3,000** |
| **Ten years of depreciation** | **$30,000** |
| **Adjusted basis (beginning basis - ten years of depreciation)** | **$72,000** |

But let's say your agent tells you that all comparable houses to the one you own have decks. In order to make your house competitive, the agent recommends you add a deck before you put your property on the market. You agree. The new deck costs you $3,000.

You've increased your adjusted basis because you've made a capital improvement to the property. Since you haven't had time to start depreciating this improvement, you may add the full cost of the deck to your adjusted basis. $72,000 + $3,000 = $75,000. This is your new adjusted gross basis in the property.

| | |
|---|---:|
| **Adjusted basis** | **$72,000** |
| **Capital improvement (new deck)** | **$3,000** |
| **Adjusted gross basis** | **$75,000** |

You sell the property for $140,000. To determine your taxable gain in the property, you subtract your selling costs and adjusted basis from the sales price.

| | |
|---|---:|
| **Sales price** | **$140,000** |
| **Selling costs** | **$10,000** |
| **Adjusted gross basis** | **$75,000** |
| **Taxable gain (sales price - selling costs - adjusted basis = $140,000 - $10,000 - $75,000)** | **$55,000** |

# Loan Amounts and Taxable Gain

But what about any loans on the property? Let's say you have a loan with an $80,000 balance. Subtracting the closing costs of $10,000 and the loan balance of $80,000 from the sales price of $140,000 produces a net to you of $50,000. So isn't the taxable gain only $50,000, not $55,000?

| | |
|---|---:|
| **Sales price** | **$140,000** |
| **Closing costs** | **$10,000** |

| | |
|---|---|
| **Loan balance** | **$80,000** |
| **Net proceeds (sales price - selling costs** | |
| **- loan balance = $140,000 - $10,000** | |
| **- $80,000)** | **$50,000** |

However, the Internal Revenue Service doesn't care about the loan. Whether you originally purchased the property with all cash or with a loan doesn't matter to them. The loan balance is treated essentially the same as cash both when the property is acquired and when the property is sold. It is ignored.

Normally this treatment of the loan balance isn't a problem. Hopefully you've been paying down your loan as fast as you've been depreciating the property, and your net proceeds and your taxable gain will be close to the same number. This means that the tax you think you'll owe on the net proceeds will be close to what you do owe on your actual taxable gain.

Let's give our example a new twist. What would happen if you had refinanced your property after owning it for eight years? You purchased your investment property for $100,000, but after owning it for eight years the value had increased to $130,000 with a loan balance of $75,000. You refinanced the property to pull out some of your equity.

Your bank was willing to give you a loan equal to 80% of the new value of $130,000, or $104,000. When you paid off the old loan balance of $75,000 plus $2,000 in closing costs, you walked away with $27,000.

| | |
|---|---|
| **New loan** | **$104,000** |
| **Closing costs on new loan** | **$2,000** |
| **Old loan** | **$75,000** |
| **Cash out (new loan - closing costs on new loan** | |
| **- old loan = $104,000 - $2,000 - $75,000)** | **$27,000** |

Did you have to pay taxes on this $27,000? No, because the Internal Revenue Service doesn't consider refinancing a property to be a taxable event. Continuing with our example, you sell your property in the tenth year for $140,000. The new loan has been paid down to $100,000. When you subtract the selling costs of $10,000 and the new loan balance from the selling price, you get net proceeds of $30,000.

| | |
|---|---|
| **Sales price** | **$140,000** |
| **Selling costs** | **$10,000** |
| **Loan balance** | **$100,000** |
| **New net proceeds (sales price - selling costs** | |
| **- loan balance = $140,000 - $10,000 - $100,000)** | **$30,000** |

Since you receive only $30,000 when you sell your property, it may seem unfair to have to pay taxes on a gain of $55,000. Remember, though, you pulled $27,000 out of the property two years ago. The Internal Revenue Service didn't tax you on that money then, but you will be taxed now based on your capital gain in the property.

Overall, the fact that the Internal Revenue Service doesn't tax you on money you pull out of a property through refinancing is actually an advantage for the investor. It's always better to pay taxes later rather than sooner as long as you remember that the tax bill will come due the day you sell the property. You must make sure you'll have enough money to pay your delayed taxes or else use a 1031 deferred tax exchange to reinvest your proceeds.

---

In a worst case scenario it's possible to sell a property and end up owing more in taxes than you receive at the closing. Let's take a look at our example again, but this time we'll say you have owned the property for twenty years. That means you've depreciated your basis in the property by another $30,000. Taking the beginning basis of $102,000 and subtracting twenty years worth of depreciation gives you an adjusted basis of $42,000.

| | |
|---|---|
| **Beginning basis** | **$102,000** |
| **Twenty years of depreciation** | **$60,000** |

**Adjusted basis ($102,000 - $60,000)**  **$42,000**

If you add the deck just before you sell the property, your adjusted basis in the property will become $45,000.

**Capital improvement (new deck)**  **$3,000**
**New adjusted basis ($42,000 + $3,000)**  **$45,000**

You've owned the property for an additional ten years and its value has increased to $200,000. Your selling costs are now $15,000. Subtracting the selling costs and the adjusted basis from the sale price gives you a taxable capital gain of $140,000.

**Sales price**  **$200,000**
**Selling costs**  **$15,000**
**Adjusted basis**  **$45,000**
**Taxable capital gain (Sales price -**
  **selling costs - adjusted basis = $200,000**
  **- $15,000 - $45,000 )**  **$140,000**

You refinanced the property with an 80% loan-to-property value loan, giving you a new loan balance of $160,000. After paying off the old loan balance of $58,000 plus closing costs on the new loan, you walked away with $100,000 cash. Half a year later you sell the property. Subtracting the selling costs and the loan balance, now $159,000, from the selling price gives you net proceeds equalling $26,000.

**Sales price**  **$200,000**
**Selling costs**  **$15,000**
**Loan balance**  **$159,000**
**Net proceeds (Sales price - selling costs**
  **- loan balance = $200,000 - $15,000**
  **- $159,000)**  **$26,000**

Since your taxable gain is $140,000 you must pay taxes on that amount. This $140,000 in gain will be taxed at two different rates. Since you have depreciated the property by $60,000, $60,000 of your total gain is considered attributable to this depreciation, and under current law is taxed at a maximum federal tax rate of 25%. You will owe $15,000 on this portion of your gain (this is the exception to the well-touted maximum capital tax rate of 20% created in the spring of 1997).

The remainder of your gain, $80,000, will be taxed at whatever capital gain tax rate applies to you. Assuming that you will incur the maximum regular capital gain tax rate of 20%, you will owe an additional $16,000. Your total federal taxes due will be $31,000.

| | |
|---|---|
| **Tax on gain attributed to depreciation** | |
| **(25% of $60,000)** | **$15,000** |
| **Tax on balance of capital gain** | |
| **(20% of $80,000)** | **$16,000** |
| **Total taxes due ($15,000 + $16,000)** | **$31,000** |

Here is where you could land in hot water. Your proceeds from selling the property will be $26,000, but you could potentially owe taxes of $31,000. Looking only at the federal taxes due and ignoring any state tax which you may also owe, you will have to come up with an extra $5,000 at tax time. If you have spent or reinvested the entire $100,000 you received when you refinanced, you may not be able to afford to sell your rental property.

---

You can't count on a real estate agent to point out a problem tax situation like the one in the previous example. An agent's job is to sell your property and to tell you what you will net without taking into consideration your tax liability. You'll need to talk with your accountant to discuss the tax angles. The moral of this story is to check your numbers on a refinanced property with a view toward taxes before you decide to sell.

Of course, if you are doing a 1031 tax deferred exchange, you will avoid the immediate problem of owing more taxes than you will net in proceeds from a sale because you'll be able to continue deferring your tax liability into the future.

If you've had an accountant doing your taxes for you, you don't have to calculate your taxable gain yourself. Call your accountant and ask what your current basis is in the property you want to sell. If you've been doing your taxes yourself, you'll have to do your own basis calculations. At the very least you may decide to hire an accountant to double-check your figures.

## To Exchange or Not to Exchange

Let's say your taxable gain when you sell a property will be only $3,000. If your combined federal, state, and local taxes are 20%, your tax burden will be $600, or the approximate cost of doing an exchange. There would be little financial advantage to doing an exchange.

However, if your gain will be $20,000, a 20% combined tax bracket would mean a tax bill of $4,000. If you plan to reinvest your proceeds in real estate, you should be doing an 1031 tax deferred exchange. The cost of hiring a qualified intermediary will be far lower than your potential tax bill. The money you save can continue to compound and grow for your benefit instead of for Uncle Sam.

## The Rules for 1031 Tax Deferred Exchanges

To have your sale of a relinquished property (or properties) and purchase of a replacement property (or properties) qualify as a 1031 tax deferred exchange, you must follow some rules listed in the tax code. The basic rules are easy to understand and we'll cover them first. If you want to do a more complicated exchange, the first set of rules may not work for you. However, the law provides for exceptions, and we'll look at those later.

As I mentioned at the beginning of this chapter you must exchange "like kind" property. This means you must exchange real property for real property. Any kind of real property will do. You can exchange a piece of vacant land for an apartment house, an apartment house for ten condominiums, or three houses for a small commercial strip mall. In Colorado water rights are also considered real property. If you get tired of tenants and think that the value of water is sure to skyrocket with the next drought, you could use a 1031 tax deferred exchange to switch your property investments into water rights.

The second basic requirement of a 1031 tax deferred exchange is that you may not receive the proceeds from the sale of your property. Someone else must hold the funds until they can be reinvested into a replacement property. You must hire a qualified intermediary to fill this role; your exchange will not be valid if you simply ask your real estate agent or a title company to hold the money for you. Legally you could demand your funds from anyone except a qualified intermediary, and since you have this right you have what is called constructive receipt of your funds.

A qualified intermediary, on the other hand, can and will legally refuse to give you your funds for a restricted period of time. You grant this power when you sign the paperwork authorizing the person or company to act as your qualified intermediary. This written agreement with the intermediary prevents you from taking possession of or exercising control of your money except as provided for by the tax code. If you eventually decide not to complete a 1031 tax deferred exchange, the code specifies when the intermediary may return your funds to you.

## Selecting a Qualified Intermediary

Finding a qualified intermediary can be as easy as looking in the phone book, but a recommendation is the better route. At this time no federal requirements, and very few state requirements, exist to govern who can or cannot call themselves qualified intermediaries. Anyone from an attorney to a real estate broker to a title or escrow company may offer to act as a 1031 tax deferred exchange intermediary.

However, there is a rule that disallows anyone who has acted in an agency position for you within the last two years to act as your qualified intermediary. For example, your real estate agent or personal lawyer would be disqualified if they have worked for you within the last two years.

You do not have to hire someone locally to act as your qualified intermediary. Many 1031 tax deferred exchange specialists offer national service. Paperwork is faxed or overnighted, and money is wired from one account to the next. Questions can be asked and answered over the phone.

---

Tax exchanges may involve only properties located inside the United States and the US Virgin Islands. Why? Because a 1031 tax deferred exchange allows you to defer federal taxes. As long as your investments stay in the United States, the Internal Revenue Service knows it will be paid taxes when and if you do sell a property without exchanging it. Money shifted into investments outside of the United States may be gone for good without any eventual receipt of taxes by the Internal Revenue Service.

---

You will want to investigate the person or institution you hire to act as your intermediary. You'll want someone with experience, and you'll want someone you can trust with your money. While it is possible to set up systems to protect yourself against the possibility of the intermediary stealing your funds such as requiring your signature to release funds, these options add costs to your basic exchange fee. In any case, you'll want to hire someone with a sterling reputation since it's possible for an intermediary to be in control of several million dollars of other people's money at any given time.

The cheapest way to avoid exposure of your money to theft is to schedule the closing date for your relinquished property and the closing date for your replacement property for the same day. Then the intermediary can arrange for your funds to be sent from one closing directly to the next closing. (You must hire an intermediary even if you are doing back-to-back closings unless you are actually exchanging your property for the seller's property, something which occurs rarely.) Having both closings on the same day allows you to neatly avoid the issue of the intermediary holding your funds for an extended period of time.

Scheduling both closings together can create problems of its own if you are exchanging into several properties. Logistics may prevent you from having all of the closings occur on the same day. Even of you do schedule all of your closings perfectly, problems may occur. You may have trouble with your loan on the replacement property, and therefore the second closing will have to be postponed while you make the lender happy. Someone else involved in one of the transactions could become ill or die. The possibilities are endless.

A workable alternative is to protect yourself by hiring someone trustworthy and with a good track record. You can and should check on what the intermediary is doing to safeguard funds in-house. If you are hiring a company to act as your qualified intermediary, at least two people in the firm should have to sign to release funds. Client funds involved in exchanges should be kept in an account segregated from the company's operating funds, and an outside certified public accountant should be doing or at least checking the financial record keeping.

# Identifying Your Replacement Properties

You must identify, that is provide a list of your potential replacement properties, within forty-five days after the sale of your relinquished property. This identification must be in writing and delivered to your qualified intermediary.

You will have to comply with certain restrictions when you identify your replacement properties. You must identify specific properties. It is not sufficient to say you will buy something located in a certain city or county or neighborhood. You must identify individual pieces of property by their specific street addresses (legal descriptions are not required).

Though you have forty-five days to identify the properties you may buy, you should try to identify them much sooner. You may identify them even before you close on your relinquished property. You should be looking for your replacement properties as soon as your relinquished property goes under contract.

Since you can change your list of identified properties up until the forty-five day deadline, you'll want to give yourself time to have each identified property inspected before the deadline expires. If the inspector finds major problems, you may redo your list and substitute a different replacement property for the one you decided was unacceptable. By identifying early you've given yourself the flexibility to change your mind.

# Identifying Replacement Properties

You must comply with rules which restrict the number of properties you may identify as potential replacement properties. If you identify three or fewer, you will qualify for a 1031 tax deferred exchange even if you eventually buy only one or two of these properties. If you identify more than three replacement properties, you must satisfy one of two additional requirements.

The first exception is when you identify replacement properties with a combined fair market value which equals or is less than 200% of the fair market value of your relinquished property.

**Fair market value of replacement property = (less than) 2 X fair market value of relinquished property**

Let's say you sell a house for $150,000. You want to buy four condominiums each worth $50,000 as your replacement properties. All properties are priced at fair market value. Will you be in compliance with the first exception to the rule which allows you to identify only three potential replacement properties?

**4 X $50,000 = $200,000**
**2 X $150,000 = $300,000**

Because the fair market value of your identified replacement properties is less than twice the fair market value of your relinquished property, this identification would be valid, even if you don't buy all four of the condominiums.

The second exception allows you to identify more than three replacement properties even when the fair market value of these properties exceeds the maximum allowed by the first exception. If you identify properties worth more than 200% of the fair market value of your relinquished property, you must close on enough identified properties to allow you to acquire 95% of their value.

Let's say you sell a house worth $200,000. If you identify four replacement properties worth $110,000 apiece, the total fair market value of the replacement properties is $440,000. Since this is more than twice the fair market value of your relinquished property (2 X $200,000 = $400,000), you must purchase properties worth 95% of the total identified replacement properties' value in order for your 1031 tax deferred exchange to be valid.

**95% of $440,000 = $418,000**

Since each property is worth $110,000, if you fail to buy even one, you will not have purchased 95% of the value of the identified replacement properties. Then none of your purchases will qualify as 1031 tax deferred exchanges, and you will owe tax on your entire gain from the sale of the relinquished property.

Does this mean you should never identify replacement properties worth more than 200% of the value of your relinquished property? Not at all. Remember, if you've identified three or fewer properties, the 95% requirement doesn't apply in the first place. Even if you only close on one property your exchange will still be valid (though you may not have managed to defer all your taxes if you failed to reinvest all of your proceeds from the relinquished property - this is covered later in this chapter).

If you have identified four or more replacement properties, then you still have a safety plan. If you schedule all of your closings for the replacement properties within the forty-five day identification limit, you'll know if any deal falls apart in time to redo your list of identified properties. You will, of course, remove that problem property from the list. The key is to schedule all of your closings within the forty-five day identification deadline.

## 180 Days to Close

No matter how many replacement properties you have identified, you have up to 180 days after selling the relinquished property to buy them. The actual guidelines say you have 180 days after the sale or until the filing of your next federal tax return, whichever occurs first, to buy your replacement properties. Sometimes, depending when you sell your relinquished property, you will have to file a tax extension if you want to use the maximum of 180 days before you close on your replacement property.

Though it's generally best to close on your replacement property or properties as quickly as possible after the sale of the relinquished property, you may need the full 180 days. You may be under contract to buy a new property, and it will take time for it to be built. Or a seller may insist on a later closing date for tax purposes. Having 180 days to close on your replacement property gives you valuable flexibility.

## Reinvesting All of Your Proceeds

If you want your exchange to be 100% tax deferred, you must comply with more requirements. You must reinvest all of your cash into the replacement property. In addition your replacement property must have a value equal or greater than the value of the relinquished property. If you do take some cash out and don't reinvest it, or if your replacement property is worth less than the relinquished property, you will owe taxes on that money.

Let's say you sell a property worth $200,000 and your taxable gain is $100,000. You have depreciated the property by $40,000. This means $40,000 of your gain will be attributed to depreciation and taxed at 25%. The remaining $60,000 will be taxed at your maximum capital gains rate.

If you take out any cash when you do an exchange, the Internal Revenue Service will calculate taxes due first at the highest rate that could apply which is the 25% on gains attributed to depreciation. Any cash you receive in excess of the depreciation you've taken will be taxed at your maximum capital gain rate.

## Carrying Over Your Basis

In the first example in this chapter we sold a house for $140,000 with an adjusted basis of $72,000. After subtracting closing costs, our taxable gain was $55,000. Let's say we use a 1031 tax deferred exchange when we purchase a new property for $180,000. What is our basis in this replacement property?

We take our taxable gain of $55,000 which we have carried over from our relinquished property and subtract it from the

$180,000 purchase price to get our starting adjusted basis, $125,000, in the new property. This means our basis in the new property is reduced by the amount of taxable gain we are protecting from taxes by doing the 1031 tax deferred exchange. If we turn around and sell the new property, the Internal Revenue Service will be paid taxes on the taxable gain which has been carried over into the new property.

The tricky question is how to approach your new depreciation schedule. There are no rules that I am aware of which define how this should be done. The theory behind a 1031 tax deferred exchange is that your investment has stayed the same and only the address has changed. This means you have already taken some depreciation on your new property and cannot depreciate based on the new improvement value. I would guess that you should subtract the amount you depreciated on the old property from the new improvement value, and then depreciate that amount.

For example, if I depreciated a total of $30,000 on the old property, and the new property has an improvement value of $150,000, then I would have $120,000 in improvements I could depreciate. But this assumes that the ratio of land to improvements is the same for both properties. The bottom line is that you will need to consult an accountant and find out what amount he or she thinks you can depreciate on the new property.

## The Reverse Exchange

You may locate the property you wish to buy before you sell your relinquished property. In this case you coud do what is known as a title holding or reverse exchange. This type of exchange got its name because your intermediary buys the replacement property (using funds provided by you) before you sell the relinquished property. The intermediary holds the replacement property until the sale of the relinguished property occurs, and then transfers title to you as part of a 1031 tax deferred exchange.

Title holding/reverse exchanges are not directly addressed in the tax codes, making these exchanges riskier. If you are audited, the Internal Revenue Service may challenge whether or not your exchange qualifies as a legitimate 1031 tax exchange. However, these types of exchanges have been audited and have passed the scrutiny of the Internal Revenue Service in the past. Therefore, many sophisticated investors have decided to do them. If this is something you would like to try, hire someone who has had experience doing title holding/reverse exchanges to help you.

## The Improvement Exchange

Sometimes you will want to exchange a property for one that is not already built. Or you may wish to purchase a property that needs extensive renovations, and you want to include the cost of those renovations in the exchange value of your replacement property. In situations like these you can provide a qualified intermediary with the funds to build or renovate your replacement property, either before or after the sale of your relinquished property. The tricky part is to make sure you close on your replacement property within the 180 day deadline.

## Contract Provisions

When you do a 1031 tax exchange, you will need the buyers and sellers involved in your various transactions to agree to sign the necessary paperwork. The 1031 tax experts who assisted me with this chapter, Andrew Ogden and Richard Levy, have generously allowed me to include in this book the contract language they suggest investors working with them use in their contracts. If you are the seller, you would add the following language in the "Additional Provisions" section of your contract.

BUYER AGREES TO COOPERATE IN AN IRC SECTION 1031 EXCHANGE BY SELLER AT NO COST OR LIABILITY

TO BUYER INCLUDING, WITHOUT LIMITATION, THE AS-SIGNMENT OF SELLER'S RIGHTS, BUT NOT SELLER'S OBLIGATIONS, UNDER THIS CONTRACT ON OR BEFORE CLOSING TO SELLER'S QUALIFIED EXCHANGE INTER-MEDIARY, (put in the name of your intermediary).

If you are the buyer, you would make the contract in the name of "(your name) and/or Assigns" and add the following language in the "Additional Provisions" section of your contract.

SELLER AGREES TO COOPERATE IN AN IRC SEC-TION 1031 EXCHANGE BY BUYER AT NO COST OR LI-ABILITY TO SELLER INCLUDING, WITHOUT LIMITA-TION, THE ASSIGNMENT OF BUYER'S RIGHTS, BUT NOT BUYER'S OBLIGATIONS, UNDER THIS CONTRACT ON OR BEFORE CLOSING TO BUYER'S QUALIFIED EX-CHANGE INTERMEDIARY, (put in the name of your interme-diary)

SELLER FURTHER ACKNOWLEDGES AND AGREES THAT, AT BUYER'S REQUEST, BUYER'S EARNEST MONEY DEPOSIT SHALL BE REFUNDED TO BUYER BY SELLER AND REPLACED WITH AN EQUAL AMOUNT OF FUNDS FROM BUYER'S QUALIFIED EXCHANGE INTER-MEDIARY AT ANY TIME AFTER ASSIGNMENT OF THIS CONTRACT TO BUYER'S QUALIFIED INTERMEDIARY."

Of course, these clauses should not be construed as tax or legal advice. They are provided here to give you an idea of the wording you could use in your contracts. You should check with your own qualified intermediary for recommended language.

You may not want to tell a seller that you are doing an ex-change. If you have passed the forty-five identification deadline, and the seller's property is one of the limited number of proper-ties you identified, the seller may conclude that you need to buy this property and that you will pay a premium for it.

The seller may be right. A premium may be cheaper than paying the taxes if your exchange falls apart, but it would be better to pay no premium at all. If you are approaching the forty-five day deadline, you may decide not to include the exchange language in your contract and trust that the seller won't balk at signing the 1031 documents at the closing.

If you do decide to include the language in order to prevent potential problems at the closing table, the seller or the seller's agent may ask how long it's been since the sale of the relinquished property. Be evasive. Say it's not been long, and change the topic.

Tell your agent to protect your interests by also being evasive. Many agents get to chatting, and before they know it, they've disclosed that you sold your relinquished property more than a month ago. Whoops. There goes your negotiating power. Do try to avoid this type of situation by lining up your properties well ahead of the identification deadline.

## Summary

In general, 1031 tax deferred exchanges are easy to do. Most exchanges involve only one or two replacement properties and avoid the more complicated rules entirely. Doing a 1031 tax deferred exchange is a wonderful way to conserve your capital for reinvestment whenever you decide to sell one of your rental properties. As long as you use an experienced qualified intermediary who can guide you through the applicable rules, all your 1031 tax deferred exchanges should be valid. By doing 1031 tax deffered exchanges, you can postpone paying capital gain taxes indefinitely.

# Appendix A - Cash Flow Worksheet

Use this worksheet to determine how much cash flow a sample house would produce if you owned it free and clear.

**Annual Income**

Projected monthly rent X number of months rented  a) _____

**Annual costs**

      Average annual maintenance     _____
      Taxes     _____
      Insurance     _____

Total Annual Expenses (a - b)     b) _____

**Annual Net Cash Flow**

Annual income - annual expenses     c) _____

## Sample Cash Flow Worksheet

**Annual Income**

Projected monthly rent X number of months rented  a) <u>12,650</u>

**Annual costs**

      Average annual maintenance     <u>1,485</u>
      Taxes     <u>1,100</u>
      Insurance     <u>360</u>

Total Annual Expenses     b) <u>2,945</u>

**Annual Net Cash Flow**

Annual income - annual expenses (a - b)     c) <u>9,705</u>

# Appendix B - Average Annual Maintenance

Use this worksheet to predict the annual maintenance costs for any given property averaged over ten years. The list of ten year expenses includes several blanks for other. Other expenses may be the cost of fencing, repairing a porch, or any other expenditure you feel a particular property will need.

## Annual Miscellaneous

Small stuff such as minor repairs and ads          a) _____

## Ten Year Expenses

Repaint exterior (may occur twice)          _____
New furnace          _____
New roof          _____
New hot water heater          _____
Repaint interior          _____
New carpet          _____
New vinyl          _____
New air conditioner          _____
Other          _____
Other          _____
Other          _____

Total Ten Year Expenses          b) _____

## Average Annual Expenses

Total ten year expenses divided by 10          c) _____

## Combined Annual Costs

Annual Miscellaneous + Average Annual (a + c)          d) _____

# Sample Average Annual Maintenance

This worksheet uses the numbers from the example in Chapter One.

## Annual Miscellaneous

Small stuff such as minor repairs and ads          a) <u>  250</u>

## Ten Year Expenses

| | |
|---|---|
| Repaint exterior | <u>3,000</u> |
| New furnace | <u>1,500</u> |
| New roof | <u>3,000</u> |
| New hot water heater | <u>  450</u> |
| Repaint interior | <u>1,250</u> |
| New carpet | <u>2,000</u> |
| New vinyl | <u>1,200</u> |
| New air conditioner | <u>    0</u> |
| Other | <u>    0</u> |
| Other | <u>    0</u> |
| Other | <u>    0</u> |

Total Ten Year Expenses          b) <u>12,350</u>

## Average Annual Expenses

Total ten year expenses divided by 10          c) <u>1,235</u>

## Combined Annual Costs

Annual Miscellaneous + Average Annual (a + c)     d) <u>1,485</u>

# Appendix C - Cash Flow per $1,000

Use this worksheet to calculate the cash flow you would receive for each thousand dollars worth of equity you have invested in a property owned free and clear.

**How Many Thousands Invested in Sample House**

Cost of sample house divided by 1,000          a) _____

**Cash Flow per $1,000 Invested**

Annual Net Cash Flow from Sample House          b) _____
Cash flow per thousand (b divided by a)          c) _____

**Value of Target Properties**

Target income          d) _____
Target total property value (d divided by c)          e) _____

# Sample Cash Flow per $1,000 Worksheet

**How Many Thousands Invested in Sample House**

Cost of sample house divided by 1,000          a) _____130

**Cash Flow per $1,000 Invested**

Annual Net Cash Flow from Sample House          b) _9,705
Cash flow per thousand (b divided by a)          c) _74.65

**Value of Target Properties**

Target income          d) _50,000
Target total property value (d divided by c)          e) _670,000

# Appendix D - Rate of Return

Purchase price                                               _____
New loan                                                     _____
Down payment (purchase price - new loan)                     _____
Previous appreciation and principal paydown                  _____
Total cash invested (closing costs + down payment
+ previous appreciation and principal paydown)               _____
Income received                                              _____
Expenses
     Taxes                                    _____
     Interest                                 _____
     Insurance                                _____
     Miscellaneous                            _____
     Total expenses                                       _____
Cash flow (income - expenses -principal paydown)   _____
Principal paydown                                            _____
Appreciation                                                 _____
Depreciation                                                 _____

**Cash flow rate of return**
Cash flow divided by total cash invested                     _____
**Principal paydown rate of return**
Principal paydown divided by total cash invested   _____
**Appreciation rate of return**
Appreciation divided by total cash invested                  _____
**Tax Savings**
Depreciation amount multiplied by your combined
federal, state, and local income tax percentage              _____

**Total rate of return**
Four rates of return added together                          _____

# Index

# Order Form

Call 1-800-833-9327 to order by credit card from the Tattered Cover Book Store. The discounts on multiple copies offered by the publisher for direct orders will not apply to 1-800 credit card orders handled by the bookstore.

Or copy and mail this order form directly to: Gemstone House Publishing, P.O. 19948, Boulder, CO 80308.

Name: _____

Address: _____

_____

City & State: _____

Zip: _____

Phone #: _____

Discount schedule when ordering direct from publisher:

| | |
|---|---|
| 1-2 books | no discount ($18.95 ea) |
| 3-4 books | 20% ($15.16 ea) |
| 5-99 books | 40% ($11.37 ea) |

For larger quantities, contact the publisher for discount.

Please send _____ copies of *Rental Houses for the Successful Small Investor* at $_____ each for a book total of $_____

Add $3.00 shipping for the first book      $___3.00___

Plus $1.00 for each additional book      $_____

Total:      $_____

Payment: _____ Check        _____ Mastercard or Visa

Card #: _____

Expiration Date: _____      Signature: _____